DATE			

809
Title

You transcendentalists make the
fatal mistake of denying education,
of sundering present from past
and future from present. These
things are indissolubly one,
the present deriving its
consciousness only from the past,
and the future drawing all its
distinctive wisdom from our
present experience.
Henry James, Sr. (1860)

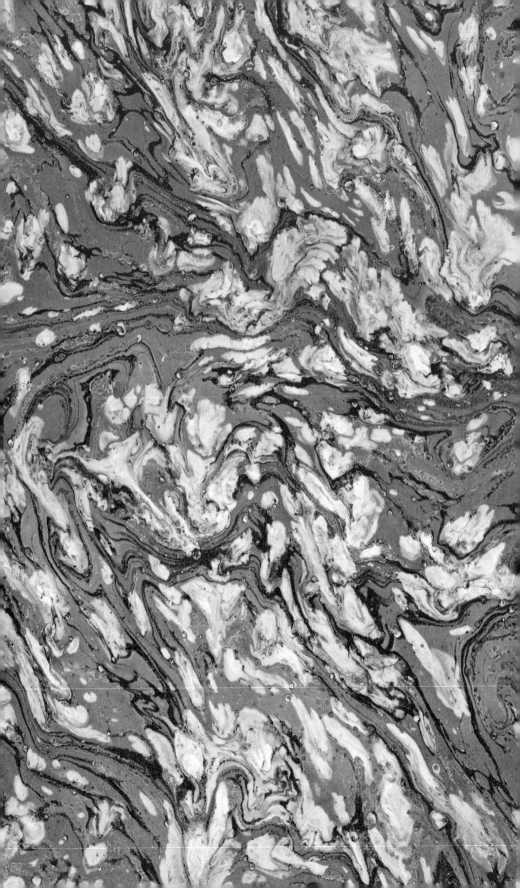

EDUCATED LIVES:

The Rise of Modern Autobiography in America

THOMAS COOLEY

OHIO STATE UNIVERSITY PRESS: COLUMBUS

Library of Congress Cataloguing in Publication Data

Cooley, Thomas, 1942–
    Educated lives.

    Includes bibliographical references and index.
    1. Autobiography.   2. American literature—History and
criticism.   I. Title.
PS169.A95C6   809   76-28952
ISBN 0-8142-0263-2

FOR SHEILA AND DAN

CONTENTS

Foreword

Emerson thought he lived in "the age of the first person singular."[1] It was, however, the generation of American writers born more or less in 1840 who actually based their work on the experience Emerson described when he wrote: "It is very unhappy, but too late to be helped, the discovery we have made that we exist. That discovery is called the Fall of Man."[2] Henry Adams, Mark Twain, W. D. Howells, Henry James, and others of a truly lapsed generation registered this unsettling discovery in numerous poems, plays, novels, essays, short stories, and historical treatises. But nowhere did they seem more painfully conscious of the self as a thing apart than in the voluminous autobiographies they wrote late in their careers from perspectives that now (unlike Emerson's or Thoreau's) seem recognizably "modern." The intention of this book is to examine some of the best, or most typical, of those autobiographies as modes of self-expression that take their narrative contours from their authors' preconceptions of the fallen self. From Henry Adams, it borrows the term "education" to describe what is here taken to be the underlying structure distinguishing the autobiographies of Adams's generation from earlier autobiographies in America. An opening chapter defines the education form by contrast with those autobiographies of "cultivation" in which Thoreau and still earlier American writers expressed a fundamentally static view of the psyche. Throughout the book, developments in the new science of psychology late in the nineteenth century are linked with parallel developments in the new autobiography, and special attention is given to Adams's, Clemens's, Howells's, and Henry James's encounters with those "lower" levels of consciousness that their pre-Freudian generation recognized but hesitated to locate beyond conscious control. A final chapter draws upon the autobiographies of Lincoln Steffens, Sherwood Anderson, and Gertrude Stein to indicate what became of the education form in the next generation.

Besides assuming that every autobiography implies a theory of human nature, this book further assumes that all autobiographies select, in Northrop Frye's words, "those events and experiences in the writer's life that go to build up an integrated pattern" and so are "inspired by a creative, and therefore fictional, impulse."[3] Thus so-called "non-fictional" narratives will be discussed with the same attention to rhetoric that we are used to bestowing upon novels and poems. It was, in fact, to attempt "readings" of significant American autobiographies that this study was originally undertaken. At the same time, however, the art of autobiography is here understood to occupy a middle ground between fiction and history. Although autobiographers enjoy a freedom so far unavailable to historians or biographers (especially in the manipulation of narrative point of view), they have not yet been set entirely free of what has happened to them. Accordingly, such accounts as some gifted American autobiographers have given of their lives are here tested against what is known from "outside" sources. Often inconsistencies in the record are considered more revealing than consensus; and always it is taken for granted that though an autobiography "inevitably" shirks the truth, as Mark Twain said, "the remorseless truth *is* there, between the lines."[4]

A few years before he lamented the fall of mankind into self-consciousness, Emerson said that friendship "must not surmise or provide for infirmity"; the infirmities of this book, however, would be still more noxious without the generous assistance that kind friends have provided. Edwin H. Cady is aware, I hope, that I have benefited more from his learned guidance than I can ever properly acknowledge. I am happy to owe an equally long-standing debt of gratitude to Terence Martin, James H. Justus, Merritt E. Lawlis, and John W. Crowley. More recently, colleagues at Ohio State have saved me many embarrassments by their expert readings of my manuscript, and it is a pleasure to name them here: William Allen, William D. Andrews, Morris Beja, Robert W. Canzoneri, Suzanne Ferguson, David O. Frantz, Julian Markels, and Charles B. Wheeler. For other forms of kindness as well as editorial advice, I especially thank Richard D. Altick, James R. Kincaid, John M. Muste, and Christian K. Zacher. I am also grateful for the support of Arthur E. Adams, Kenneth Burrows, Robert S. Demorest, Timothy Dykstra, Kenita Floyd, John B. Gabel, Douglas Haneline, June Johnson, Weldon A. Kefauver, Jane Ott, Margaret M. Patton, and Thomas Woodson. Through a quarter of research leave and a grant-in-aid, I have received welcome assistance from the Department of English and the College of Humanities of the Ohio State University; the National Endowment for the Humanities awarded me a much appreciated summer stipend in 1972.

The support I have received from my wife, an attorney, has been both lateral and subjacent.

1. William H. Gilman and Alfred R. Ferguson, eds., *The Journals and Miscellaneous Notebooks of Ralph Waldo Emerson* (Cambridge, Mass.: Harvard University Press, 1960–73), 3:70.

2. Edward Waldo Emerson, ed., *The Complete Works of Ralph Waldo Emerson* (Boston: Houghton Mifflin, 1903–4), 3:75.

3. *Anatomy of Criticism: Four Essays* (Princeton, N.J.: Princeton University Press, 1957), p. 307.

4. Henry Nash Smith and William M. Gibson, eds., *Mark Twain-Howells Letters: The Correspondence of Samuel L. Clemens and William D. Howells, 1872–1910* (Cambridge, Mass.: Harvard University Press, 1960), p. 782.

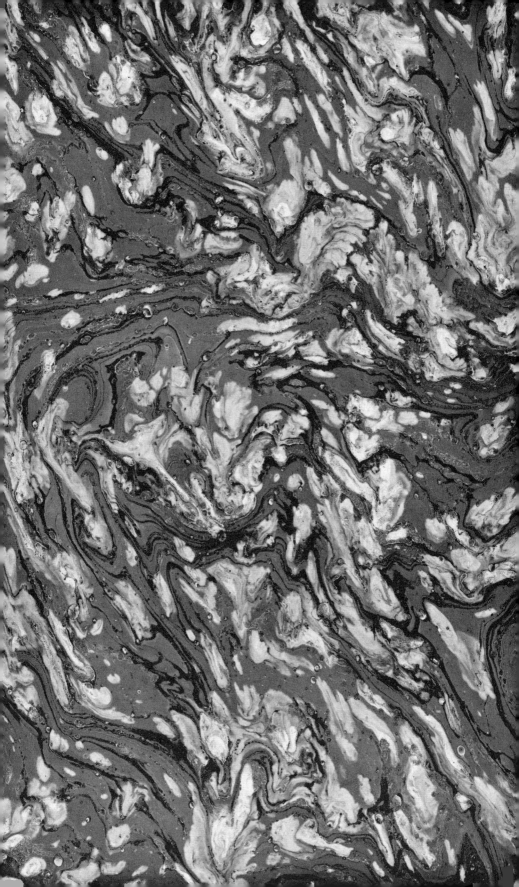

1

Origins of the Self
Autobiography in America before 1865

> The type is cheap, dirt cheap. It's the variation from the type that is the character, the individual, the valuable and venerable personality.—W. D. Howells, *The Shadow of a Dream* (1890)

> The Intuitive Philosophy has been censured . . . by the Sensualistic School for contemplating the mind only in its maturity, with no sufficient allowance for the results of previous conditions upon it,—for the effects of growth.—John Bascom (1881)

In 1797 a contributor to the British *Monthly Review* wrote of Isaac Disraeli's *Miscellanies* (1796): "The next dissertation concerns *Diaries, and Self-Biography*. We are doubtful whether the latter word be legitimate: it is not very usual in English to employ hybrid words partly Saxon and partly Greek." The unnamed reviewer, almost certainly the linguist William Taylor of Norwich, offered "autobiography" as a thoroughbred Greek replacement for "Self-Biography" even though it seemed to him "pedantic." Pedantic or not, Taylor's coinage survived, of course, first appearing in the title of an American book in the second quarter of the nineteenth century.[1] (The author of the most influential of all American autobiographies, the *Autobiography of Benjamin Franklin*, thought of his narrative as his "memoirs.")

As suggested by the welter of terms that authors and readers have adopted to describe it—"memoirs," "personal narrative," "life," "confession," "reminiscence," "spiritual autobiography," and two new terms to be applied here, "cultivation" and "education"—the narrative genre we now call "autobiography" is actually a cluster of genres whose early history in America remains largely unwritten. If we focus for the moment upon the roles of their authors, however, it is nevertheless possible to indicate in a general way the basic forms of autobiographical writing in which Americans first expressed themselves and in which modern American autobiography had its origins.

Well over one-third of all autobiographies written in this country before 1850 were religious narratives, including spiritual autobiographies, reminiscences of missionary work, and the life stories of clergymen. Many of these were published by sectarian presses, already thriving in the early decades of the nineteenth century, or by job printers receptive to pious causes and the relatively dependable bill-paying habits of religious groups. Not all early religious autobiographies were as well-written or theologically sophisticated as Jonathan Edwards's "Personal Narrative," with its discovery of joy in God's sovereignty, "shewing Mercy on whom he will shew Mercy, and hardening and eternally damning whom he will."[2] But a shrewd comment by W. D. Howells in his "Editor's Easy Chair" can remind us that the brief autobiography of that "mighty theologue" was but one culmination of a tradition well established in America when Edwards wrote his life in the early 1740s. Drawing on long acquaintance with the form as author, reader, and reviewer, Howells speculated that autobiography "seems supremely the Christian contribution to the forms of literaturing."[3] This is a notable anticipation of more recent criticism which holds that autobiographical writing enjoyed great popularity in Puritan America as an aid to spiritual exercise. In autobiographies and journals, the pious could record lives of soul-searching for the enlightenment of others and, at the same time, take inventory of their spiritual stock. Cotton Mather had said that "frequent Self-Examination, is the duty and the prudence, of all that would *know themselves*, or would not *lose themselves*;[4] and such advice was taken seriously enough in America that a later puritan, Henry Adams, observed in his *Education* how "the highest intelligence known to history had drowned itself in the reflection of its own thought."[5]

Many Americans followed Mather in practicing introspection "to find out, the points, wherein we are to *amend our ways*"; but readers of the second most popular autobiographies after the religious narratives looked for instruction to the unhappy examples of others.[6] These were the "confessions" (often ghost-written) of notorious thieves, murderers, rapists, and counterfeiters. Usually under twenty-five pages long and published in the same locale and year of the subject's execution, criminal narratives were circulated ostensibly to discourage lawbreaking. The original "Confessions of Nat Turner" (1832), for example, abounds in righteous indignation. Turner's confessor, Thomas Gray, declares of the insurrectionists that "the hand of retributive justice has overtaken them, and not one that was known to be concerned has escaped."[7] Most readers, however, probably bought Gray's fast-selling pamphlet as much for scenes like this from the massacre as for the author's moralizing:

> As we pushed on to the house, I discovered some one running round the garden, and thinking it was some of the white family, I pursued, but finding it was a servant girl belonging to the house, I returned to commence the work of death; but they whom I left had not been idle: all the family were already murdered, but Mrs. Whitehead and her daughter Margaret. As I came round to the door I saw Will pulling Mrs. Whitehead out of the house, and at the step he nearly severed her head from her body with his broad axe. Miss Margaret, when I discovered her, had concealed herself in the corner formed by the projection of the cellar cap from the house; on my approach, she fled, but was soon overtaken, and after repeated blows with a sword, I killed her by a blow over the head with a fencerail.[8]

Through such passages, criminal narratives titillated public curiosity and retailed the same peculiar combination of moralism and sensationalism that marks a book like the "autobiography" of Daniel Defoe's Moll Flanders.

Three related modes of autobiographical writing in early America could lay less claim to redeeming moral value than the confessions. The largest of these—accounts of their experiences by naval officers, merchantmen, impressed sailors, privateers, and whalemen—is notable chiefly as the tradition that produced Richard Henry Dana's *Two Years before the Mast* (1840) and that influenced Herman Melville through such narratives as *Life and Remarkable Adventures of Israel R. Potter* (1824) and Henry James Mercier's *Life in a Man of War* (1841).[9] The success of *Typee* (1846) and Melville's frequent later attempts to capitalize on it, indicate just how popular first-person accounts of shipboard life had become by the 1840s. The popularity of a similar tradition of autobiographies by soldiers and civilians swept up in war is attested by James Fenimore Cooper's *The Spy* (1823). Whether or not Harvey Birch is modeled on the real-life Enoch Crosby, Crosby's memoirs as told to H. L. Barnum (*The Spy Unmasked*, 1828) reversed the usual pattern of indebtedness by drawing heavily on Cooper's novel. Slightly less numerous than sea narratives, such military lives capitalized on the same demand for martial exploits that sustained the group of autobiographies usually called "captivity narratives" and consisting of the reminiscences of hostages (or simply sojourners) amidst Indians, pirates, political enemies, or criminals.

When we remember that the victims in captivity stories were often women and that the military lives included such titles as Eliza Webb's *The Female Marine* (1818) and Lenora Siddons's *The Female Warrior* (1843), we can better understand the true appeal of a subspecies of autobiography before 1850 that constituted one of the earliest distinctively feminist forms of literature in America. A clear indication of the makeup of the American reading public in the nineteenth century, these can only be described as narratives of female sufferings and domestic tragedy. Some, such as Elizabeth Munro Fisher's *Memoirs* (1810), appear genuinely concerned to reveal the immorality of domestic cruelty. Others in this vein, however, wander somewhat from hearth and home. Mary Marshall's "Life and Sufferings" (1847) recounts the inescapable difficulties of marrying a man who was to become a Shaker. *The Life and Sufferings of Miss Emma Cole* (2d ed., 1844) tells of a servant girl who escaped her duties in Maine, fell in with pirates, but managed to return and get married. And *The Cabin Boy Wife* (1840) recalls how Mrs. Ellen Stephens sought out her faithless husband by dressing as a boy and working in the cabins of Mississippi riverboats. Such narratives satisfied the reader's appetite for high adventure in a culture where out-and-out fiction was held morally suspect. In a climate officially hostile to "frivolous" literature, autobiographies (or domestic romances disguised as autobiographies) could enjoy a place even on sparse bookshelves because they professed to record not what writers imagined or dreamed but what had actually happened to living witnesses. For a people who defined reality as the plain, the common, the universally apprehendable, nothing could be more legitimate than a firsthand account of one's experience.

A final subspecies of autobiography in early America addressed itself primarily to the reader's social consciousness. The pioneering *Narrative of the Uncommon Suffering and Deliverance of Briton Hammon, a Negro Man* (1760) was followed by perhaps as many as several hundred autobiographies of fugitive and former slaves. At its height in the decades immediately preceding the Civil War, the slave narrative tradition emerged through a collaboration between "authors" and supporters of the abolition movement to whom the narratives were often "told." The Boston Anti-Slavery Society, for example, published no fewer than seven editions of Frederick Douglass's *Life* between 1845 and 1849; and in 1879, the editors of the *Life* of Josiah Henson, reputed model for Harriet Beecher Stowe's Uncle Tom, claimed that the book had sold 100,000 copies since its appearance thirty years before.[10] (Their initial success, however, did not prevent slave narratives from lapsing into almost total obscurity during the first half of the twentieth century. Although they have been retrieved in the last few years, Booker T. Washington's *Story of My Life and Work* alone remained in print in 1954; and it survived, according to Arna Bontemps, "by disguising itself as something other than part of the genre in which it was first presented.")[11]

Such then, in bare outline, were the principal native varieties of autobiography available to Americans before 1850.[12] It is true, of course, that autobiographical forms were hardly the exclusive property of clergymen, criminals, seamen, soldiers, beleaguered women, and slaves. An occasional physician, farmer, or frontiersman (including Daniel Boone and Davy Crockett) and now and then a lawyer, politician, businessman, or actor contributed his life story to a curious public as well. Moreover, two historical turns of events brought in new strains after midcentury. The gold rush and the settlement of Texas yielded, in the fifties, a rich crop of narratives about life in the far West by miners, hunters, and settlers, including one Edward Wilson, whose autobiography captured the myth of California in its title —*The Golden Land* (1852). And the end of hostilities in 1865 opened the way for such war recollections as the *Century*'s remarkable "Battles and Leaders" series and U. S. Grant's *Memoirs* (1885–86). Indeed, Americans of all persuasions seemed bent upon generating autobiographies in ever increasing numbers. Between 1850 and 1865, financiers, educators, social reformers, and writers (notably Thoreau)—not to mention a smattering of dwarfs, mental patients, and reformed drunkards—joined the usual clergymen and criminals to turn out in fifteen years almost as many examples of autobiographical writing as this country had achieved in the previous two hundred years of its literary history. But though the new diversity gave promise of the new autobiography soon to emerge, for the time being it was promise only. Drastic shifts in the way Americans defined themselves (and hence the autobiographer's role) were still largely in the future.

When the definitive history of autobiography in early America comes to be written, it will no doubt describe a far greater variety of persons, professions, and forms than any suggested here. The chances are, however, that early American autobiographers will still seem basically united in their differences. For the human psychology on which their narratives were based changed little in essentials from the time of the first Mather's emigration to Massachusetts Bay until well after the publication of James McCosh's *Intuitions of the Mind Investigated* in 1860. Before 1865, American psychology was uniformly a faculty psychology set forth in frequently interchangeable paradigms in dozens of imported textbooks and American imitations. To be sure, the textbooks left considerable room for disagreement. Mental philosophers questioned which specific faculties belonged in which categories, variously explained how stimuli register in the mind, and argued about the exact number of its capacities. Different texts incorporated differences in emphasis, method, and attitude. And the Scottish Common Sense philosophy, bringing what was to become in American colleges almost a national psychology as well as an official metaphysic, appeared to revolutionize American mental philosophy by adopting a threefold division of the mind that departed from the bipartite model Jonathan Edwards had found more in accord with his doctrine of moral necessity.

The innovations of the Scots amounted, however, to little more than adaptations of the old system. The "new" faculty psychology took hold so thoroughly in America because Americans had always thought of the mind in terms of faculties— as suggested by the immense popularity in this country of phrenology, the pseudo-science of locating faculties posited by the Scots in specific areas of the brain. On the whole, uniformity of opinion continued to outweigh individual differences; and even if one philosopher disagreed with another on the precise configuration of the mind, he nevertheless assumed that his formulation applied to all men, regardless of variations in background, training, or inheritance.

This underlying unity in the old psychology was given its classic statement by William James, the American who did most to upset it. James's essay in tribute to the psychic research of Frederic Myers (1901) first observed that "the history of mental science" is marked by "diverse tendencies among its several cultivators," and then it went on to say:

> Until quite recently all psychology, whether animistic or associationistic, was written on classic-academic lines. The consequence was that the human mind, as it is figured in this literature, was largely an abstraction. Its normal adult traits were recognized. A sort of sunlit terrace was exhibited on which it took its exercise. But where that terrace stopped, the mind stopped; and there was nothing farther left to tell of in this kind of philosophy but the brain and the other physical facts of nature on the one hand, and the absolute metaphysical ground of the universe on the other.[13]

All this was changed by the advent of experimental psychology in the second half of the nineteenth century and by the forces of cultural upheaval that Henry Adams studied in all their "multiplicity." But the overwhelming uniformity of assumptions about the makeup of the human mind that earlier informed "classic-academic" psychology may be seen to inform even such apparently different narratives as the two best autobiographies written in America prior to 1865.

On their surfaces, two works could not appear less alike than Franklin's *Autobiography* and Thoreau's account of his life at Walden Pond. The *Autobiography* seems based on a limited, almost scholastic, conception of the self and its proper role that is very much at odds with Thoreau's expansive view. The modern meaning of the word *invent* obscures the fact that the "archetypal" American inventor was actually a relatively late "ectype" (good Puritan term) of the man of invention described in the following passage, which Perry Miller has called "an epitome of the Puritan mind":

> . . . The *Genesis* of every thing is Gods, and man must see the rules of Art, therefore man must see them from singulars, by *analy-*

sis: . . . in this respect is this Art of reason called Invention, namely as he is sent by God to find out these things in his creatures;
now if man must find them out with this act of his eye of reason,
then is it fitly called invention. . . .[14]

One aspect of the Puritan mind revealed in this homily by Alexander Richardson is its affinity for typology. The Puritan who discerned correspondences between the "singulars" of his personal
experience and the grand design of God's providential plan took
for granted that his individual life recapitulated and thus exemplified the life of every man on the road to salvation. Hence
G. A. Starr's contention that early American spiritual autobiographies are essentially alike: the central event is conversion;
every prior event looks toward this great transformation, and
every subsequent event follows from it.[15]

Richardson's commentary also shed light on the Puritan conception of the role of the artist. It was essentially imitative. To
learn any art, the student had to seek the rudiments piecemeal
in the creation, then combine them into general principles. This
was a process of discovery rather than an act of creation, because when a man "invented" anything, whether in the field of
rhetoric or animal husbandry, he merely compounded elements
that already existed; and though he might arrange the fruits of
analysis into clusters, he could not bring new fruits into being
—for "the *Genesis* of every thing is Gods." Perceive a need; devise a plan for meeting it; prepare the people's minds (usually
by writing); then collect funds, initiate the project, and watch it
become a going concern: these were the quintessential rules of
conduct that Franklin the public servant pieced together over a
busy lifetime of applying Reason to the data of experience. And
these celebrated "means" were as much his inventions as bifo-
cals and the Franklin stove. The supreme example in the *Autobiography*, his plan for attaining moral perfection, was just another application of Franklin's faith in rules, discipline, and
method; limiting the province of human knowledge to what Reason could comprehend, his schema nonetheless assumed there

was nothing within that province that invention (the application of Reason) could not accomplish.

The art of invention as practiced by Franklin was to lose ground in America in the second quarter of the nineteenth century with the rise of the romantic movement. Emerson, "the winged Franklin," recognized a contrast between his own and the earlier Franklin's views on the proper function of the self when he jotted in his notebook: "Transcendentalism says, the Man is all. The world can be reeled off any stick indifferently. Franklin says, the tools: riches, old age, land, health; the tools. . . . A master *and* tools,—is the lesson I read in every shop and farm and library. There must be both."[16] Emerson was here making Franklin out to be more concerned with means (as opposed to ends) and himself less devoted to "the Man" than the career of either always warranted. Emerson was mistaken when he accused Franklin of aiming "in general at nothing higher than vulgar Utilitarianism."[17] Like D. H. Lawrence after him, Emerson did Franklin the disservice of ignoring his essential piety. But Emerson was right to distinguish between men of "talent" like the inventive Franklin and the man of "genius" Emerson and Thoreau so much admired. Conceiving genius as the stirring of divinity in the "active soul," Emerson defined its function to be the "transmuting" of "life into truth."[18] The American scholar of the Phi Beta Kappa address "received into him the world around; brooded thereon; gave it the new arrangement of his own mind, and uttered it again."[19] From this belief in the creative function of human consciousness, transcendentalism derived its organic theory of poetry; and it also derived a theory of history and autobiography that suggests why Henry Adams felt Emerson's teachings to be hopelessly "naif": "We are always coming up with the emphatic facts of history in our private experience and verifying them here," said Emerson. "All history becomes subjective; in other words there is properly no history, only biography."[20]

As an Emersonian seer and a Wilberforce dedicated to emancipating the West Indian provinces of his neighbors' minds, Thoreau assumed in *Walden* a creative potential that Franklin would have found presumptuous if not blasphemous. For all the undeniable differences between the two men and their books, however, Franklin and Thoreau approached questions of human identity on the common ground best suggested by citing a figure who stood between them historically: the proto-transcendentalist, Sampson Reed.

Reed's *Observations on the Growth of the Mind* (1826) was devoted to variations on the theme that "a man cannot be other than what he is," and it set forth an organic theory of consciousness: "The mind must grow, not from external accretion, but from an internal principle. Much may be done by others in aid of its development; but in all that is done, it should not be forgotten, that even from its earliest infancy, it possesses a character . . . which *should be* respected, and *cannot* be destroyed."[21] This notion of the inviolate ego was to become the theoretical basis of the educational doctrine that Bronson Alcott called "personalism" and that inspired the Temple School experiment, Alcott's *Human Culture* (1836), and Horace Bushnell's *Christian Nurture* (1847). It was also the basic idea behind Thoreau's metaphors of growth in *Walden*. Thoreau addressed the essential man (as Emerson addressed the whole man) because he believed that character was like the seed in his bean field. Inherent in the child, it should be tended and strengthened; but it could not be altered in any primary way. Thoreau's own doctrine of simplicity, simplicity, simplicity would expose the constant self to cultivation so that it might be nurtured to the healthy maturity that is the goal of enlightened husbandry. "I want," says the narrator of *Walden*, "the flower and fruit of a man; that some fragrance be wafted over from him to me, and some ripeness flavor our intercourse."[22]

This is why *Walden* does not conform with the expectation set forth in Roy Pascal's *Design and Truth in Autobiography*. One expects from autobiography, Pascal writes, "a totality rather than a quintessence; and even if . . . an experience gives the personality a new dimension, a turn, the autobiography must embed it in a long process."[23] Thoreau's view of character as an essence prevented him from portraying it as a "totality," and the artistic economy of his narrative demanded a scrupulous weeding out of unnecessary biographical details. Hence Thoreau's decision to concentrate his entire life in a single year. And hence, too, the basic similarity between *Walden* and Franklin's *Autobiography*, a book that advised young people to cultivate moral perfection virtue by virtue because "him who, having a garden to weed, does not attempt to eradicate all the bad herbs at once . . . but works on one of the beds at a time."[24]

Since Franklin's belief in character as a constant is merely implied in the *Autobiography* and Thoreau's is stated and restated through several elaborate metaphors, some readers have argued that the protean Franklin conceived no essential identity for himself. Robert Sayre attributes what he sees as the formlessness of the *Autobiography* to just this deficiency. For Franklin, he writes, "self-teaching did not mean conclusions but repeated new beginnings." "The problem Franklin unconsciously illustrated," we are told, "was the problem of the man whose life and character was one of change and discontinuity."[25] Franklin was a better craftsman with a more unified personality than Sayre would admit, however. Far from telling a story in which past and future are disjointed, Franklin's narrator begins his personal narrative by selecting events from his early history that reveal the adult in embryo. From an abundant family tree, he chooses to mention ancestors who embodied qualities in common with those of their illustrious descendant. The great-great-grandfather who concealed an English Bible beneath the cover of a joint stool displayed the ingenuity that ran in the Franklin bloodline. The uncle, Thomas Franklin, who qualified himself as a scrivener and "became a considerable man in the country affairs," exhibited the nephew's public-spiritedness.[26]

And Josiah Franklin, prudential adviser to "leading men," showed the discretion and good judgment that his son inherited.[27]

Similarly, many of Franklin's anecdotes of childhood experiences are intended to display ways in which the child was father to the man. Because "it shows an early projecting public spirit," he delights in the escapade in which he led several boys to construct a wharf by filling a salt marsh with stone from a nearby building site.[28] He remembers too the occasion on which his father took him to see various tradesmen at their work, for it "has ever since been a pleasure to me to see good workmen handle their tools."[29] He refers to the books he read, including Defoe's *Essay on Projects* and Mather's *Essays to Do Good*, because they "perhaps gave me a turn of thinking that had an influence on some of the principal future events of my life."[30] And he gratefully recalls a friend who brought the first customer to his newly opened print shop because this timely favor made him always ready in later years to assist youthful beginners. Even the changes in his narrator—from kindly father to avuncular moralist to self-publicist—brought about as a result of Franklin's composing the *Autobiography* over a period of twenty years only momentarily obscure the unity of personality they ultimately confirm. From his "unlikely beginnings" to his achievements as commissioner to London for the colony of Pennsylvania, Franklin portrays himself as a consistently exemplary figure whose industry secures wealth (part 1), whose wealth secures virtue (part 2), and whose virtue secures fame (parts 3 and 4). The whole book, in short, verifies the assertion that the long first section is intended to illustrate: "I had, therefore, a tolerable character to begin the world with; I valued it properly and determined to preserve it."[31]

If we recall that character is the basic commodity in the "economy" of both writers, even Franklin's plan of moral discipline does not seem so alien in spirit to the detailed audit of the cost of his hut with which Thoreau only half parodied Franklin's method. Both the *Autobiography* and *Walden* may be regarded as character-building manuals written by men who already knew themselves surely enough to instruct others in the art of self-definition. (Thoreau does not discover himself in the pages of *Walden*; that discovery had come as part of the experiment *Walden* reconstructs long after the fact.) Assuming character to express an "internal principle," both imbued their fictionalized selves with traits "fit to be imitated" (as Franklin said). Thus both composed what might be termed narratives of "cultivation" rather than "education"—that is, stories about fulfilling the self's innate capacities rather than stories, like *The Education of Henry Adams*, of conforming to external forces or of failing to conform.

By presenting their readers with models of self-cultivation, Franklin and Thoreau merged their individual talents with a literary tradition that stretched at least as far back as Saint Augustine's *Confessions*. A more immediate source of their narratives of cultivation, however, was the work of Jean Jacques Rousseau. When he hoped to prepare Emile to take his proper place in society, Rousseau resembled Franklin, the great projector and public servant, more closely than the essentially anti-social Thoreau. But Emile's training, unlike prevailing educational doctrine as Rousseau saw it, was also designed to encourage self-expression of the sort Thoreau later fostered when he advised every man to follow the bent of his own genius. Emile was to receive an education that would strengthen his personal capacities instead of stifling them. As a carefully cultivated individualist, he would then be in a position to reform society even as he entered it. Extravagantly applied, such a plan of human culture could produce a figure like the hero of Rousseau's own *Confessions*, a book that Henry Adams rejected as a model for autobiographical writing in the twentieth century because of its inveterate egoism.

Applied to the development of fictional characters, the educational theories of Rousseau and others helped produce the youthful protagonists of such *Bildungsromane* as Goethe's *Wil-*

helm Meister's Apprenticeship (1795–96), Stendhal's *The Red and the Black* (1830), and Balzac's *Père Goriot* (1834). The author of every *Bildungsroman* in the nineteenth century was hardly so concerned as Goethe to equate self-fulfillment with the acquisition of a social role. Dickens, for example, was often goaded into social criticism because his little heroes could not find places for themselves within, or even on the outskirts of, society. Generally, however, these writers agreed upon the primacy of the inner man. The German term *Bildung*, as Susanne Howe has defined it, referred to "organic development according to inner capacity."[32]

Franklin's *Autobiography*, with its long first section devoted to a would-be tradesman's apprenticeship, and *Walden*, an account of the mastery of his vocation by a "surveyor" of nature, are equivalents in the autobiographical mode of the novel of apprenticeship or "formation." Both Franklin's plan for achieving moral perfection and Thoreau's opening chapter on economy (the management of life-time) may be seen as ideals of *Bildung* that assume not only that the self is defined by inner principles but that those principles can be cultivated by programs of self-discipline equally applicable to many different selves.

When Emerson declared his to be "the age of the first person singular" and Thoreau asked "of every writer, first or last, a simple and sincere account of his own life," they were celebrating the individual man in his creative aspect as Franklin celebrated him in his rational aspect.[33] The transcendentalists liberated the imagination in a culture that traditionally distrusted that faculty. But they did not seek to alter the age-old view of the healthy adult mind as a collection of faculties acting in concert. Despite its worship of the inviolate ego, transcendentalism fostered the same paradox that A. O. Lovejoy long ago ascribed to the rationalism of the enlightenment. Without contradicting himself, said Lovejoy, the rationalist (Benjamin Franklin, for example) could cite as guides to truth both the individual and the *consensus gentium* because he assumed all individuals to be "fundamentally alike, and because this uniform element in them is the only important element."[34] Or, as Emerson put the matter: "To believe your own thought, to believe that what is true for you in your private heart is true for all men,—that is genius."[35] This spirit was so basic to American transcendentalism that even the colossal egoist Walt Whitman could not speak of the separate man without uttering "the word Democratic, the word En-Masse": "I celebrate myself, and sing myself, / And what I assume you shall assume, / For every atom belonging to me as good belongs to you."[36]

Members of the literary generation after Whitman's could not be so confident of their sameness. Life seemed eccentric rather than concentric; and the self appeared to be shaped not from within but from without. Those forces of cultural upheaval that Henry Adams signified under the term "multiplicity"—vast new forms of physical power, a complicated technology, the move to the cities, burgeoning population, collectivism in government and business, new roles for women, mass literacy, and that phenomenon so puzzling to Adams, the disappearance of religion—appeared to control the American of the late nineteenth century more than he controlled them. Thoreau had scarcely lived in a golden age of unity forever lost to the new generation; but the illusion of unity, particularly unity of the self, became increasingly difficult to sustain in a period when unprecedented changes were undermining traditional sources of stability and belief. Instead of transcending circumstance, Henry Adams's manikin seemed to live in a world that was moving too fast and that no longer answered to anyone's conceptions, even in imagination.

Among the altered conditions that contributed to new ways of thinking and writing about the self in America after the Civil War, perhaps none was more formative than the rise of modern psychology. The "genetic" theories of human development popularized in America by J. Mark Baldwin, G. Stanley Hall, and others denied the long-standing belief, as Sampson Reed formulated it, that the "mind of the infant contains within itself the first rudiments of all that will be hereafter, and needs nothing but expansion; as the leaves and branches and fruit of a tree are said to exist in the seed from which it springs."[37] Instead of teaching that character is inviolable, the psychologists spoke of human nature as Howells does in *A Hazard of New Fortunes* (1890): "I suppose I should have to say that we didn't change at all. We develop. There's the making of several characters in each of us; we *are* each several characters, and sometimes this character has the lead in us, and sometimes that."[38]

According to the new theories, each period of growth in a human life constituted a distinct phase of development; infancy, childhood, and adolescence came to be seen as discrete, though connected, stages in a long process. Thus children were no longer regarded as the miniature adults pictured in "primitive" American paintings but were thought to have the unique urges and codes, in effect the unique culture, captured in the boy-books and children's magazines of the period. Whereas Thoreau had advised his mature readers to retain a childlike freshness of vision uncorrupted by civilization, Howells, Clemens, Thomas Bailey Aldrich, George W. Peck, and Frank Stockton savored the "badness" of childhood as a primitive instinct irretrievably *lost* to adults. Each epoch of an individual's personal history brought changes that made the organism in one stage of development distinct from the same organism in prior and subsequent stages. When the organism happened to be Henry Adams, it professed to see no connections at all—only change and discontinuity.

In practice, of course, Americans did not always rigidly distinguish between identity as something innate and essentially changeless and identity as the shifting deposit of a continuing process of adaptation. They often confounded the two views as in *Pudd'nhead Wilson*, where Clemens hammers home the dictum that training is everything and simultaneously "proves" that one's identity is as indelible as his fingerprints. Even many professional psychologists and philosophers resisted changes that were revolutionizing their own fields. As late as 1886, when he brought out a two-volume "Psychology" along the old lines, James McCosh was still actively preaching the doctrine that the mind of a Princeton student is essentially the mind of Adam (after the Fall, of course); and in the same year, Borden P. Bowne published an *Introduction to Psychological Theory* in which he stated confidently that "the mental facts remain what they always were. Their likenesses and differences and essential nature would not be changed if physiology were supreme."[39]

In the following year, however, with the first issue of the *American Journal of Psychology*, edited by G. Stanley Hall, and the appearance of G. T. Ladd's *Elements of Physiological Psychology*, "physiology" was well on its way to supremacy. And "then it was," according to Edwin G. Boring, "that the new theory of evolution was taken over in energetic America with an enthusiasm that in some savants, like Stanley Hall, amounted to religious fervor."[40] Drawn together by a concern for genesis and development, William James, Hall, Ladd, J. Mark Baldwin, James McKeen Cattell, John Dewey, and a number of lesser figures imbued American psychology with a "functionalism" unmatched in any other country. Psychology became the study not of mental faculties like reason and intuition but of mental functions—the study of mind in use.

The new psychologists re-defined the basic function of the human mind as something quite different from what Thoreau and other philosophical idealists had taken it to be. Instead of an instrument for penetrating the surfaces of life to apprehend truth within or beyond nature, mind became to these men an organ of adaptation, altering environment when possible, being altered by it in turn—as the struggle for survival demanded. Functional psychology shifted, in Boring's words, "from the description of the generalized mind to the assessment of personal capacities in the successful adjustment of the individual to his environment."[41]

Where the new psychology parted company most drastically with the old, William James made clear, was in its certain assurance "that consciousness has no essential unity."[42] For James, consciousness "aggregates and dissipates, and what we call normal consciousness,—the 'Human Mind' of classic psychology,— is not even typical, but only one case out of thousands."[43] Thoreau might awake and feel a dawn in him; but he was never, in the functionalists' view, quite the same man of the morning before. For the functionalists, consciousness was cumulative rather than recurrent and identity, therefore, not innate but situational.

Yet the ever changing "stream of thought" remained sensibly continuous: Peter could wake in the morning and know that he was Peter and not Paul.[44] The conscious self, as William James defined it, was "a *Thought*, at each moment different from that of the last moment, but *appropriative* of the latter, together with all that the latter called its own."[45] This definition was almost identical to James's definition of memory: "*the knowledge of an event, or fact, . . . with the additional consciousness that we have thought or experienced it before.*"[46] Memory is the chief resource of any autobiographer, and the generation that defined self-awareness as an exercise in perpetual recollection was doubly susceptible to the kind of autobiography written by Henry Adams. The task of the education form, as Adams established it for his age, was to discover continuity among the selves one had assumed over a lifetime. Identity in a "pluralistic" universe depended upon the perception of continuity, and an artful life necessarily yielded evidence of linear design—like a river or a stream.

Henry James, Sr., recognized this necessity long before his first son stated it as a principle of psychology. Writing to a "survivor" of transcendentalism, he protested that men are not "born to all the faculty they shall ever have, like ducks." Transcendentalism made, the elder James said, "the fatal mistake of denying education, of sundering present from past and future from present. These things are indissolubly one, the present deriving its consciousness only from the past, and the future drawing all its distinctive wisdom from our present experience."[47]

Henry Adams denied that education brought wisdom, but he too felt the urge to link past, present, and future when recollecting his personal life. Inclined to conceive of the self as the product of constant change, Adams and his generation were forced by their abdication of religious faith to search their self-recollections for universal values and lasting hope. Lacking God, the American of the late nineteenth century had little but the self to fall back on. These are the contradictions that characterize the American experience after 1865. They are at the heart of Adams's *Education*, a good starting place, therefore, for examining the conventions and compulsions informing the new autobiography.

1. The earliest listing in Louis Kaplan's *A Bibliography of American Autobiographies* (Madison: University of Wisconsin Press, 1961) with the word in the title is *The Autobiography of Thomas Shepard, The Celebrated Minister of Cambridge, N. E.* (Boston, 1832). William Taylor reviewed Disraeli's *Miscellanies* in the *Monthly Review*, 2d ser., 24 (1797): 374–79.

2. Samuel Hopkins, *The Life and Character of the Late Reverend Mr. Jonathan Edwards* (Boston: S. Kneeland, 1765), p. 25. The first published edition of Edwards's autobiography appears on pp. 23–39.

3. *Harper's Monthly Magazine* 119 (October 1909): 796.

4. *Bonifacius: An Essay upon the Good . . .* , ed. David Levin (Cambridge, Mass.: Harvard University Press, 1966), p. 35. Usually known by the title *Essays to Do Good*, Mather's *Bonifacius* was first published in Boston in 1710.

5. *The Education of Henry Adams* (1907; first public edition Boston and New York: Houghton Mifflin, 1918), p. 432.

6. Levin, *Bonifacius*, p. 35.

7. The pamphlet that inspired William Styron's "meditation on history" was first published in Richmond, Va., early in the year following Turner's execution in 1831. Citations here are to an 1861 edition (rpt. Miami, Fla.: Mnemosyne Publishing), p. 11.

8. *The Confessions of Nat Turner*, p. 7.

9. In the few instances where first editions of autobiographies cited here have not been available or positively identifiable as first editions, the dates of publication are those given in Kaplan's *A Bibliography of American Autobiographies*.

10. These publication figures are taken from Arna Bontemps, *Great Slave Narratives* (Boston: Beacon Press, 1969), p. xviii.

11. Ibid., p. vii.

12. The foregoing statistics are based partly on a reordering in chronological sequence of the items in Louis Kaplan's *A Bibliography of American Autobiographies*. Despite its more than 6,300 entries, Kaplan's list is far from exhaustive, and it cites editions available to the editor and his assistants, not necessarily first editions. Nonetheless, this standard bibliography is a reliable guide to relative proportions among the various traditions of autobiographical writing in America through the middle of the twentieth century.

13. *Memories and Studies* (New York: Longman's, Green, 1911), pp. 147–49.

14. *The New England Mind: The Seventeenth Century* (New York: Macmillan, 1939), p. 162.

15. *Defoe and Spiritual Autobiography* (Princeton: Princeton University Press, 1965), pp. 39–41. For the argument, however, that American spiritual autobiographies of the seventeenth and eighteenth centuries "ought not to be categorized exclusively" as conversion narratives, see Daniel B. Shea, Jr., *Spiritual Autobiography in Early America* (Princeton: Princeton University Press, 1968), pp. xi–xii. Franklin's portrait of himself might be said to depart from Puritan models because its standards of self-examination are outward and social rather than inward and divine. It is true that Franklin (in the famous wheelbarrow scene, for example) is concerned about appearances; but Franklin was anxious to *be* virtuous as well as to *seem* so. His "Articles of Belief and Acts of Religion" showed that Franklin held himself to inner standards of piety, and he further resembled Puritan spiritual autobiographers in assuming that a good life was exemplary.

16. Edward Waldo Emerson and Waldo Emerson Forbes, eds., *Journals of Ralph Waldo Emerson* (Boston and New York: Houghton Mifflin, 1909–14), 7:268.

17. Stephen E. Whicher et al., *The Early Lectures of Ralph Waldo Emerson* (Cambridge, Mass.: Harvard University Press, 1959–72), 2:67.

18. Alfred R. Ferguson and Robert E. Spiller, eds., *The Collected Works of Ralph Waldo Emerson* (Cambridge, Mass.: Harvard University Press, 1971), 1:56, 55.

19. Ibid., p. 55.

20. Edward Waldo Emerson, ed., *The Complete Works of Ralph Waldo Emerson* (Boston: Houghton Mifflin, 1903–4), 2:9–10.

21. *Observations on the Growth of the Mind; With Remarks on Some Other Subjects*, 3d ed. (Boston: Otis Clapp, 1838; rpt. Gainesville: Scholars' Facsimiles and Reprints, 1970), p. 31.

22. Bradford Torrey, ed., *The Writings of Henry David Thoreau* (Boston and New York: Houghton Mifflin, 1906), 2:85.

23. (London: Routledge & Kegan Paul, 1960), p. 12.

24. Max Farrand, ed., *The Autobiography of Benjamin Franklin: A Restoration of a "Fair Copy"* (Berkeley and Los Angeles: University of California Press, 1949), p. 104. Why the associates who completed Farrand's work chose "autobiography" over Franklin's word, "memoirs," is not explained in the introductory material either to this book or to Farrand's *Benjamin Franklin's Memoirs: Parallel Text Edition* (Berkeley and Los Angeles: University of California Press, 1949).

25. *The Examined Self* (Princeton: Princeton University Press, 1964), pp. 13, 16.

26. *Autobiography*, p. 6.

27. Ibid., p. 13.

28. Ibid., p. 12.

29. Ibid., p. 15.

30. Ibid., p. 16.

31. Ibid., p. 72.

32. *Wilhelm Meister and His English Kinsmen: Apprentices to Life* (New York: Columbia University Press, 1930), p. 24.

33. Thoreau, *Writings*, 2:4.

34. *Essays in the History of Ideas* (Baltimore: Johns Hopkins University Press, 1948), p. 82.

35. *Complete Works*, 2:45.

36. Harold Blodgett and Sculley Bradley, eds., *Leaves of Grass: Comprehensive Reader's Edition* (New York: Norton, 1968), p. 28.

37. Elizabeth Peabody, ed., *Aesthetic Papers* (Boston: The Editor, 1849), pp. 58–59. The entire text of Reed's essay, "Genius," appears on pp. 58–64.

38. George Warren Arms, ed., *A Hazard of New Fortunes* (New York: E. P. Dutton, 1952), p. 540. The first hardback edition was published by Harper and Bros. (New York, 1890).

39. (New York: American Book Co., 1886), p. vi. For President McCosh's views on Princeton students, see Howard Mumford Jones, *The Age of Energy* (New York: Viking, 1971), p. 22.

40. *A History of Experimental Psychology*, 2d ed. (New York: Appleton-Century-Crofts, 1950), p. 508.

41. Ibid., p. 507.

42. *Memories and Studies*, p. 163.

43. Ibid., p. 163.

44. In the 1890 edition of James's *Principles of Psychology* (New York: Henry Holt and Co.), the popular ninth chapter was entitled, "The Stream of

Thought"; in the *Psychology: Briefer Course* (1892), this chapter was re-numbered "twelve" and given the title, "The Stream of Consciousness."

45.   *The Principles of Psychology*, 1:401.

46.   Ibid., p. 648.

47.   Quoted in Frederick W. Dupee, ed., *Henry James: Autobiography* (New York: Criterion Books, 1956), pp. 375–76.

2

The Dissolving Man
Henry Adams

> We can justify any apologia simply by calling life a successive rejection of personalities. . . . So we do sell our souls: paying them away to history in little installments. It isn't so much to pay for eyes clear enough to see past the fiction of continuity, the fiction of cause and effect, the fiction of a humanized history endowed with "reason."—Thomas Pynchon, *V* (1963)

I

For years after the private printing of the *Education* in 1907, Henry Adams continued to fret over the book's shortcomings. My "art fails of its effect," he told Elizabeth Cameron in one of the requests for imprimatur sent out to friends named in the text. To the historian James Ford Rhodes, he disparaged the book as a "centipede," dragging its thirty-five sections laboriously along. It was mere "drivel," he warned a geologist friend. And to Ferris Greenslet, whose persistence finally landed for Houghton Mifflin the first public edition of the *Education*, Adams wrote simply: "My idea of what it should be proved beyond my powers."[1]

The autobiographer's dissatisfaction ranged over a multiplicity of complaints, from the starkness of the American scene ("You can't get your contrasts and backgrounds") to his own and his audience's well-bred composure ("It will not make a scandal even if generally read").[2] But Adams's misgivings, exaggerated in the letters, tended to coalesce around a single imperfection as he came to regard the *Education* "chiefly as a literary experiment."[3] The "point on which the author failed to please himself," he explained in the posthumous preface signed by Senator Henry Cabot Lodge but written by Adams, "was the usual one of literary form." By comparison with Saint Augustine, a model autobiographer whose unified vision made him "a great artist," Adams felt himself to be a "small" artist indeed.[4]

Adams was never much in danger, however, of succumbing to the example of the other autobiographer whose famous *Confessions* occupied him in the second preface to the *Education*. In a letter to Barrett Wendell, Adams divulged what he had learned not only from Saint Augustine but also from Jean Jacques Rousseau. "We have all three," Adams wrote, "undertaken to do what cannot be successfully done—mix narrative and didactic purpose and style." Augustine lapsed into pure didacticism toward the end of his *Confessions*, but Rousseau's narrative failed "wholly in didactic result" because it degenerated "into still less artistic egoism."[5]

This pitfall Adams had taken great pains to avoid. He did not need the negative example of Rousseau's "monument of warning against the Ego" to be reminded of the hazard of personal exhibitionism (p. x). All his life Adams had the New England aristocrat's distaste for public exposure except on his own terms. Moreover, after reading biographies that eviscerated his friends, Adams resolved, as he advised Henry James, to "take" his own life in his own way "to prevent biographers from taking it in theirs."[6] How well the autobiographer succeeded in masking his subject may be gathered by the decision of biographer Ernest Samuels to "put aside *The Education* as a primary source, referring to it only occasionally to indicate the sort of reservations that need to be made."[7] The *Education* was the "shield of protection" Adams intended it to be.[8] The personal question with which the book opens, "What was he?—where was he going?" (p. 21), gave way to an unstated, impersonal question that might be phrased, What was the world like—where was it going? And the perennial inquiry of the professional historian, Where had it been? According to one reading, Adams's narrative veered off into history and left personal history behind.

Certainly it showed that one did not need to make a spectacle of oneself in order to accomplish Rousseau's major objective. Whereas Rousseau had begun his *Confessions* by blatantly daring the reader to say, "I was a better man!"—a passage Adams quoted prominently in his preface—the "manikin" began by claiming to be almost beneath contempt. No one stood lower —except the distinguished people who found dwarfed versions of themselves in this American social register of the century. Adams's ironic self-effacement was thus a more subtle version of Rousseau's challenge, and anyone who took the manikin's estimate of himself at face value was disqualified from membership in the elite band of survivors who constituted for Adams the true reading public.

There was, however, little false modesty behind Adams's pretense of failure. In Adams's view, only an ignoramus hopelessly blind to the multiplicity around him pretended to march unimpeded toward some glorious, predetermined goal. To the groping student, the majority of Americans seemed "a crowd of men . . . ignorant that there is a thing called ignorance; who have forgotten how to amuse themselves; who cannot even understand that they are bored" (p. 297). Like Augustine's, Adams's Socratic irony held up ignorance as a wisdom this benighted multitude would do well to adopt. In an age that had abdicated belief to the point of losing even the ability to worship money, everyone was small if rightly seen; and Adams showed what a superior man was reduced to by casting himself in the anonymity of a type—the bumbling seeker to whose literary ancestors the *Education* constantly alludes. Shunning

Rousseau's egotism and shrinking to anti-heroic proportions, Adams was adopting the tactics of the embattled realists, who had exposed the folly of trying to live a romance. The expansive "I" of Thoreau's transcendent individualism had no place in the work of a man who could say, "The ego may pass in a letter or a diary, but not in a serious book."[9]

The *Education* was a serious book. It was Adams's serious didactic purpose, in fact, that almost defeated the storyteller in the closing pages of his narrative. This often-quoted letter to William James specifies where Adams thought his art had fallen short:

> Did you ever read the Confessions of St. Augustine, or of Cardinal de Retz, or of Rousseau, or of Benvenuto Cellini, or even of my dear Gibbon? Of them all, I think St. Augustine alone has an idea of literary form,—a notion of writing a story with an end and object, not for the sake of the object, but for the form, like a romance. I have worked ten years to satisfy myself that the thing cannot be done today.[10]

As usual with his protestations of failure, Adams lapsed into overstatement; he had followed Augustine's example more closely than he would have us believe. But Adams could not finally duplicate Augustine's *Confessions* without falsifying his experience of his own times. In writing the *Education*, he discovered firsthand the inaccessibility of Augustine's form "today." Indeed, Adams's anti-romance achieved an Augustinian end and object only by overturning the train of logic Adams's own form had set in motion. Having worked backward from the confession model, where the basic convention is an ending that spiritually "justifies" the sinner by lifting the load of guilt he has borne previously, Adams claimed to base his autobiography on the more modern premise that education is an ongoing process of trying to adapt to one's environment. Such an assumption called for an open-ended narrative whose "hero" is schooled in flux and change. Through the first nineteen chapters or so, the *Education* seems precisely this; but Adams's compulsion to give his life a satisfying shape—"like a romance" —caused him to impose upon his persona's career the same shape and pattern he was coming to impose upon history. The closing chapters setting forth the historian's dynamic theory amount to a formal justification, though not in spiritual terms, of the halting nature of the pilgrim's earlier "progress." Adams's ultimate complaint with his artistry was not that he failed to give the *Education* a discernible form but that the universe failed to yield entirely to its precision.

II

As we might expect from the work of a former professor of rhetoric, Saint Augustine's *Confessions* is constructed on a principle of dialectic. Augustine's tendency to arrive at order through warring contraries shows up in his narrator's fondness for dialogue, in his antithetical style, and in a recurring contrast between images of light and darkness. Augustine's greatest influence upon *The Education of Henry Adams*, however, arises from his handling of "plot." The plan, stated before God, by which he arranged the events of his narrative, called for Augustine's "re-collecting myself out of my dissipation, in which I was torn to pieces, while, turned away from Thee the One, I lost myself among many vanities."[11] Anticipating the turning but focusing upon the dissipation, Augustine's art required him to wallow in a host of sins and heresies and to delay the climactic moment of spiritual conversion while hinting that it was ever drawing closer: "I all but came to a resolve," he says repeatedly in effect. "I all but did it, yet I did it not."[12]

The object of Augustine's "romance" was, of course, to dispel such tensions. Young Augustine, "divided amid times" and following a life of "dispersion," had to be brought to unity with God, for only then could the Many flow together in the One (Augustine's great theme) and the necessity of dialectic ultimately be denied.[13] The resolution came in book eight, just after a morality debate in which Augustine's persona "hung in suspense" between his old mistresses and "the chaste dignity of Continence."[14] To many modern readers and to Henry Adams, however, the *Confessions* is most engaging in the early books, before Augustine "re-collects" his scattered identity from dissipation.

Certainly it was the dramatic potential of dialectic, demonstrated by Augustine's art of suspense, that Adams imitated in the structure of the *Education*, beginning with his earliest memories of childhood. Five paragraphs into the *Education*, Adams recalls the color yellow, learned by sitting on a kitchen floor in strong sunlight, and the taste of a baked apple served to him after the crisis of a month-long bout with scarlet fever. Looking back, he is mildly surprised that the first-remembered sensations of life were pleasurable. Adams the autobiographer would have been better served by some telling contrast in his first memories, such as that between the strikingly beautiful peach blossoms and pathetic drowning man that epitomized a serious division in the psyche of W. D. Howells. Almost as if to correct the deficiency, the narrator adds that his third recollection was the discomfort of being bundled into heavy blankets for moving to a new house. The season was midwinter, and the memory prompts Adams to describe the New England climate:

> The chief charm of New England was harshness of contrasts and extremes of sensibility—a cold that froze the blood, and a heat that boiled it. . . . The violence of the contrast was real and made the strongest motive of education. The double exterior [of] nature gave life its relative values. Winter and summer, cold and heat, town and country, force and freedom, marked two modes of life and thought, balanced like lobes of the brain. (P. 7)

As Adams's references to the seasons multiply, the qualities associated with each fall into a pattern of opposition. Winter comes to represent "confinement, school, rule, discipline"; "restraint, law, unity"; "the desire to escape and go free." Summer, on the other hand, stands for "liberty, diversity, outlawry"; "tropical license"; "the multiplicity of nature" (pp. 8–9).

Such contrasts suggest that the seasons, which figure so prominently in the *Education*, serve as emblems not so much of restraint and release as of disjuncture. Thus Adams tells us, still in chapter 1:

> The bearing of the two seasons on the education of Henry Adams was no fancy; it was the most decisive force he ever knew; it ran through life, and made the division between its perplexing, warring, irreconcilable problems, irreducible opposites, with growing emphasis to the last year of study. From earliest childhood the boy was accustomed to feel that, for him, life was double. (P. 9)

Much later in the *Education*, Adams will express this same sense of overwhelming division in apparently orthodox Christian terms:

> He could not escape it; politics or science, the lesson was the same, and at every step it blocked his path whichever way he turned. He found it in politics; he ran against it in science; he struck it in everyday life, as though he were still Adam in the Garden of Eden between God who was unity, and Satan who was complexity, with no means of deciding which was truth. (P. 397)

This is Manichean heresy coming from the autobiographer who once said that Augustine's *Confessions* "stated the Manichean doctrine more forcibly than the orthodox," and the rest of Adams's autobiography is equally heretical.[15] Assuming duality, tension, and ambiguity from the start, Adams's persona everywhere encounters "irreducible opposites": winter and summer, union and secession, Adams blood and Johnson blood, unity and multiplicity, the One and the Many.

Since the *Education* is built on a rhetoric of suspension like the opening books of its model, Adams constructs the first twenty chapters as a series of puzzles that confound his persona much as Augustine was confounded by that "most entangled enigma," the problem of time.[16] Thus in chapter 6

Adams fails to foresee that Rome "was mechanically piling up conundrum after conundrum in his educational path, which seemed unconnected but that he had got to connect" (p. 90). A chapter later he is mystified by the double "treason" of the southern states' break with the Union and of Charles Sumner's break with the Free Soil party. Then follow the five chapters that recount Adams's diplomatic education while serving as unofficial secretary to his father, Lincoln's minister to England. From his entire experience in the legation, Adams can draw a conclusion that is no conclusion at all: he reaches his twenty-sixth birthday having been tossed "between the horns of successive dilemmas" and having learned only that he lacks the "power of earning five dollars in any occupation" (p. 194).

While the manikin dabbles along in pursuit of a suitable profession, the enigmas continue to swarm; and in chapter 15 Adams's quest for a career leads to the most perplexing quandary he has yet encountered. Hoping to consolidate his gains from the publication of an essay on John Smith, Adams jumps at the chance to introduce a new edition of Sir Charles Lyell's *Principles of Geology* to an American audience. The result in the *Education* is a witty account of Adams's personal disillusionment with Darwinian thought and a revealing glimpse of the impact of evolutionism on the late nineteenth century. When Adams begins to study Lyell, he professes the will to believe in evolutionism; but he concludes by believing only in "Evolution that did not evolve; Uniformity that was not uniform; and Selection that did not select" (p. 231).

Politics is equally disillusioning. Through the first fifteen chapters, the *Education* shows the moribund condition of "moral" statesmanship in the tradition of John Adams and John Quincy Adams. The loss of the retired sixth president in 1848 marks one death spasm, and the failure of the Free Soil party to gain decisive power signals another. President Grant is made to scuttle the old statesmanship forever. The Grant years as Adams portrays them amount to a Darwinian "Free Fight" in which natural selection generates friction (and finally chaos) rather than any improvement in the species. The fulfillment of Grant's promise of "order" is a political disorder so extreme as to mark a turning point in American history: "The system of 1789 had broken down, and with it the eighteenth-century fabric of *a priori*, or moral, principles. Politicians had tacitly given it up. Grant's administration marked the avowal" (pp. 280–81). Instead of providing "some great generalization which would finish one's clamor to be educated," Adams's education among contraries has challenged the very possibility of such fixed standards as those of the eighteenth century that he began life by accepting (p. 224). Far from progressing on a straight line, his experience is coming to describe a broken series of successively intensified phases. To coincide with the shape of history, the manikin's life lacks only a disruption of personal experience corresponding to the political disorder of Washington under Grant, and that disruption comes in the chapter appropriately entitled "Chaos."

The death of Adams's sister Louisa from tetanus provides "the sum and term of education" (p. 287). By coincidence, Louisa Kuhn's death on July thirteenth had been followed on the fourteenth by the French order to mobilize troops in what became the Franco-Prussian War of 1870. Adams interprets the war as the world's attempt to mimic the delirium of his grief. The summer ends by disclosing to him "the most intimate personal tragedy, and the most terrific political convulsion he had ever known or was likely to know" (p. 291). History and personal history in Adams's narrative take on the common shape of nightmares governed only by the natural law of lawlessness.

Adams will not rest content with this conclusion, however. So far his autobiography has brilliantly borne out that fundamental premise which *The Education of Henry Adams*, perhaps more than any other book, helped establish as the basic convention of the education form: so far it has defined life for the manikin as an endless process of becoming. Education in any final sense is impossible; life proceeds toward no dramatic resolution beyond which everything falls miraculously into place. To the author of "The Rule of Phase Applied to History," however, this was a disturbing prospect. Written shortly after the *Education*, the "Rule" returned to a proposition more in keeping with Adams's eighteenth-century heritage: "That which is infinitely formless must produce form."[17] This is the conclusion Adams will foist upon his personal narrative just as it is the conclusion he will foist upon history. Autobiography will carry him to it at last in chapters 33 and ·34; already in chapter 19 Adams is looking forward to the One while claiming to see only the Many. And henceforth his narrative will subtly take its shape from Adams's phase rule.

In "The Rule of Phase Applied to History," Adams defined the key term *phase* to mean *equilibrium* and noted that "every equilibrium, or phase, begins and ends with what is called a critical point, at which, under a given change of temperature or pressure, a mutation occurs into another phase."[18] As the birthdate of the dynamo, Adams theorized, the year 1870 was one such critical point between the mechanical and electric phases of Western history. The next, "ethereal" phase, when all motion would cease, was frighteningly near at hand.[19]

When we remember that the author of the first part of the *Education* was already formulating these ideas, the traumas of 1869–70 seem equivalent to "a given change of temperature or pressure" designed to bring about the mutation of Adams's life "into a new phase." This is the argument implicit in Adams's recurrent images of drift and in his reference to Gibbon. It is Gibbon's guiding presence in Rome that leads Adams to the historical puzzle under which all the other puzzles of his narrative are subsumed: the inapplicability of historical laws at the crossroads of Western civilization. "Rome could not be fitted into an orderly, middle-class, Bostonian, systematic scheme of evolution. No law of progress applied to it. Not even time-sequences—the last refuge of helpless historians—had value for it" (p. 91). In Adams's view, "not an inch" had been gained by Gibbon or anyone else "towards explaining the Fall" (p. 91). The empire should have lasted forever, yet Rome fell. Decline followed rise, but no known historical method can supply links between the two. In effect, Adams is saying that the historian who tries to impose cyclical patterns upon the chaos of Western history is reduced to sketching arcs of circles that refuse to be connected, that the evolutionist who draws a line to describe it will find his line broken by inexplicable gaps, and that neither takes into account the effect of sudden changes in a world accounted anything but uniformitarian by Adams's long experience of its upheavals. To gain his inch and succeed Gibbon, therefore, Adams sees the necessity of leaping.

Taking sequence as the *sine qua non* of history (and of education), Adams requires a metaphor that will explain the breaks in historical sequence ignored by conventional linear and cyclical theories. In the dynamic theory to be stated at the close of the *Education*, he will seize on the image of a perfect comet, and in the "Rule" he will emphasize the vaporization of water as a model. But that essay will also refer to the flow of water from a mountain range through innumerable streams and channels, reaching ultimate solution in the ocean. It is in part by this metaphor—of a current disturbed by waves but drifting unbroken to the ocean, where it ceases to flow—that Adams carries forward his persona's adventures to the year 1870. And this metaphor is clearly intended to link the persona's career with the concept of historical phases. Thus Adams says of himself at the end of the years in England: "He was in a fair way to do himself lasting harm, floundering between worlds passed and worlds coming, which had a habit of crushing men who stayed too long at the points of contact" (p. 83). And again at the end of the chapter on British eccentricity: "He was in dead-water, and the parti-colored, fantastic cranks swam about his boat, as though he were the ancient mariner, and they saurians of the prime" (p. 193). The "dead-water" refers both to the persona's stalled career and to the condition of Europe: "He might dream, but he could not foretell, the suddenness with which the old Europe, with England in its wake, was to vanish in 1870" (p. 193).

Adams the narrator can foretell, of course, and so prepares us for the approach of that fateful year. When the former secretary returns to America in 1868, he is described as a "survivor from the fifties," "a flotsam or jetsam of wreckage" (p. 238). In postwar Washington he finds everyone "mixed up and jumbled together in a sort of tidal slack-water" (p. 254). A "tidal wave of expectation" awaits Grant's assumption of power (p. 255). And after the shock of Grant's failure to appoint a reform cabinet, Adams asks on behalf of his younger self, "What course could he sail next?" (p. 263). When the persona has been launched for a year on the unexpected new course of teaching medieval history to Harvard undergraduates, Adams brings the first part of the *Education* to a close by contrasting the shape of the persona's life to date with the "straight line" of his friend Clarence King's career: "Adams's life, past or future, was a succession of violent breaks or waves, with no base at all" (p. 312). Through the imagery of drift, Adams has brought the manikin's life story to the same "conclusion" the assistant professor of history foists upon his subject: "In essence incoherent and immoral, history had either to be taught as such—or falsified" (p. 301).

When Adams's persona appears again "twenty years after" (chapter 21), very little seems to have changed despite the traumas that in 1869–70 seemed as shocking as new forces would have been to Lyell's uniformitarian geology. The persona is still drifting, albeit below the surface in what Adams liked to call his "posthumous" life; and the country, still in "slack-water," is lulled beyond caring whether to elect Cleveland or Harrison in 1892 (p. 325). Except for learning to ride a bicycle, Adams rouses himself to new life only so far as to state the puzzle that will occupy him for the rest of the book: "As

the Niagara was to the Teutonic—as 1860 was to 1890—so the
Teutonic and 1890 must be to the next term—and then?" (p. 319).
Otherwise, Adams evokes a sense of torpor that brings all activity to a standstill and makes the new epoch heralded in the
preceding chapter seem another of the persona's miscalcula-
tions.

By recurring to images of drift, however, Adams is not so
much denying as confirming the influence of his phase theory
on the form of the *Education*. Although the "Rule of Phase
Applied to History" mentions a critical *point* between phases,
Adams usually hesitates to fix sharp boundaries. The "Rule"
suggests 1870 as one possible date for dividing the mechanical
from the electric phase; 1900 is another. The ethereal phase
may end in 1921, or it may last till 2025. Given the vast scale
of Adams's inquiry, such differences are "negligible."[20] In the
Education, the convulsions of 1870 mark only the *close* of one
phase in personal and public history; another succession of
minor shocks and another great crisis must occur before the
next phase is pronounced fully under way. Adams's researches
at the time of writing the second half of the *Education* had led
him to adopt 1900 as the first year of the new era. And since
Adams differentiates but two phases in his life—one typified by
his experience before 1870 and the other characterized by his
life after 1900—the narrator of the *Education* must minimize this
thirty-year gap or else dull the distinction between his principal
terms. The break in Adams's record, however regrettable to the
biographer interested in the years of Adams's marriage and
professional career, merely follows the internal logic of the autobiographer's narrative. The manikin's personal history must
again follow the broken line of public history until he discovers
a means of connecting the apparently disconnected elements of
both. In chapter 21 he can say only, "Life had been cut in halves,
and the old half had passed away, education and all, leaving
no stock to graft on" (p. 317).

After the stifling calm of 1892 and "for the first time since

1870," Adams senses the winds of change in chapter 22 (p. 338). The financial panic of 1893 throws the country into another convulsion, and the adoption of the single gold standard re-commits America to a capitalistic economy. Pondering beneath Richard Hunt's dome like Gibbon on the steps of Ara Coeli, Adams discovers another "breach of continuity—a rupture in historical sequence" (p. 340). Previously accounted failures by conventional standards of success, Adams's friends seem finally to be coming into their own. If the trend is real, it will profoundly affect Adams's "personal universe" (p. 340). For the moment, he cannot be sure. The Chicago Exposition demonstrates the energy potential of America. It remains to be seen whether that energy will be channelled in a desirable direction. For the time being, Adams seeks the "next term" of his equation from the grave.

Further defying the conventional limitations of a form that (in contrast to biography) has no place for the protagonist's death, Adams prolongs his posthumous existence as part of the strategy to divide his history into two distinct phases, the second yet to come. After the shocks of 1893, he continues in chapter 23 to pursue ignorance in the silence of oblivion, telescoping the events of nearly five years into a few pages because they serve only "for connecting the nineteenth and twentieth centuries" (p. 346). Even the threat of war with Spain fails to resurrect him. On the whole, he is most content when burying himself in the medieval cathedrals of Normandy.

It is not until war actually erupts that Adams shows the first signs of new life. He rejoices to see England, old antagonist of the Adams family, frightened into the American camp; and though he claims not to rejoice, he has the satisfaction of seeing his friend John Hay called home to be secretary of state. For the first time, the historian thinks he perceives "a sense of possible purpose working itself out in history" (p. 363). America is expanding her influence; the Civil War and Grant have slipped into the distant past. Despite the new Gibbon's gloomy tendency to recall the fate of an earlier empire, education takes a significant turn. Adams begins "the practice of his final profession," the exercise in "triangulation" that will lead to the writing of *Mont-Saint-Michel and Chartres* and the *Education*; having discovered the ultimate puzzle, he will find his method in chapter 25 (p. 369).

When the new century opens, Adams is studying the Paris Exposition of 1900. Soon to re-avow his role as quester (this time by comparing himself to Sir Lancelot), he enters the great hall of machines, a modern Chapel Perilous where the dynamo translates steam power into electricity. This is a leap between physical phases so mysterious as to be explained only by an act of faith; but it is not so startling a breach as that between the world of Adams's experience before 1870 and the twentieth-century world of the dynamo, X-rays, and radium. Self-generating and supersensual like divinity, these forces break the historian's "historical neck" by negating all previous ways of thinking (p. 382). Adams is jolted back to life in "a new universe which had no common scale of measurement with the old" (p. 381). Entering the hall of machines, he has left the mechanical phase of history behind to enter the electric phase at last.

Since the new forces have made the old formulas obsolete, Adams must try a desperate experiment if he is now to discover continuity between the Virgin and the dynamo and between the eras they represent. Reduced to his last resources, he will try to link up the contraries he has encountered by measuring "their attraction on his own mind": he must deal with them "as convertible, reversible, interchangeable attractions on thought" (p. 383). On parallel but distinct courses until now, history and personal history have become indistinguishable. Henceforth, very little happens in the *Education*, and didacticism gradually takes over from the narrative impulse. Giving up the role of Lancelot to become a befuddled Teufelsdröckh in the following chapters, Adams will test the hypothesis that history and autobiography tend toward "complexity, and multiplicity, and even contradiction" (p. 397). Adams has finally found his drift, or rather, "the drift found the seeker, and slowly swept him forward and back, with a steady progress oceanwards" (p. 426).

In the service of Virgin and dynamo, Adams hits on the idea of applying the laws of mechanics to history. Viewed in this context, the two occult powers seem attracting rather than repulsive forces; and by declaring them to be so, Adams takes the first step toward working acceleration into his theory. Once a unit of measurement is found, the scientific historian will almost be ready to set his system in motion. Psychology supplies a unit by showing Adams that the modern psyche has been fragmented into discrete personalities set against each other by drives beyond conscious control. Adams will measure the progress of history toward this view of man as so many deviations from a more unified view and will take for his base the century 1150–1250, "when man held the highest idea of himself as a unit in a unified universe" (pp. 434–35). Before making a full statement of his theory, Adams must confirm only his suspicion about the direction in which history moves.

When, in "The Grammar of Science," Adams discovers scientists themselves calling chaos "the law of nature" and order "the dream of man," he is prepared to assert that intractable Western culture is moving at a constantly accelerating rate in all directions toward greater diversity (p. 451). In order to help it along with yet another cataclysm, Adams deftly distorts history to make the assassination of the Russian minister of the interior in July 1904 seem a failure of the Virgin's grace and "the last word of Progress" (p. 472). A desperate act of self-assertion is now in order as Adams's persona, like the earlier Teufelsdröckh, realizes that his America is here or nowhere. Proclaiming every man's responsibility "to account to himself for himself somehow," the manikin vows to devise "a formula of his own for his universe" (p. 472). The dynamic theory that follows is Adams's version of Carlyle's Everlasting Yea and the final lesson of the manikin's education.

III

Again and again Adams's misgivings about the form of the *Education* harked back to this last portion of the narrative. "I found," he confided to Barrett Wendell, "that a narrative style was so incompatible with a didactic or scientific style, that I had to write a long supplementary chapter to explain in scientific terms what I could not put into narration without ruining the narrative."[21] By concluding with a large block of theorizing, Adams felt he had followed Saint Augustine into physics overwhelmed in metaphysics and narrative overwhelmed in didactic purpose and style. This failure in narration, such as it was, stemmed from Adams's compulsive need to resolve the dramatic tension that held his persona suspended between irreducible opposites and so to force a synthesis from his dialectic. Adams claimed to have failed in this as well.

The *Education* fell below Augustine's *Confessions*, he said, in that the great artist "had worked from multiplicity to unity, while he, like a small one, had to reverse the method and work back from unity to multiplicity" (pp. vii–viii). A theory that saw history leaping into successive phases of increasingly rapid motion was subject to the objection Adams himself had raised playfully in the role of Conservative Christian Anarchist: it might reduce history to formulaic unity, but "the unity was chaos" (p. 406). For although Adams's theory argued that the movement of history reached a stable equilibrium in its final phase, it held the new equilibrium to be the opposite of synthesis. "The Rule of Phase Applied to History" made it clear that the ultimate relation of elements in Adams's system was nearly infinite separation.[22] All motion would cease because all items in the system drew so far apart that attraction and repulsion faded out. Such then is the "synthesis" toward which Adams's dialectic tends, and it is a far cry from the endpoint of dialectic for Augustine. Renouncing the Manichean heresy of his youth, Augustine had learned to view the universe as an interrelated hierarchy instead of a field of polar opposites. Thus Christ became for him a mediator between God above and the Many below; and after a life beset by "tumultuous varieties," Augustine could say, "I flow together unto Thee, purged and molten in the fire of Thy love."[23]

Adams could not follow Augustine so far as to take unity on faith and give up dialectic altogether. Yet Adams felt the appeal of a mediator strongly enough to pursue the Virgin throughout the churches of France, and his search for a "formula" showed that this "creature of our poor old Calvinistic, St. Augustinian fathers," as Adams called himself, could not suppress a compulsion to seek moral order if not moral absolutes.[24] The vein of pessimistic determinism in Adams's thought had to contend with an opposing philosophical idealism that willed a semblance of order upon the disorder of his experience. In this, as several critics have remarked, Adams resembled Mark Twain. Ernest Samuels describes the syndrome this way:

> The contradiction between the obsessive pose of pessimism and the lurking residue of optimism was but part of the web of contradictions that Adams, like Mark Twain, had always perceived in himself. The air of desperate urgency in the face of an always imminent-seeming disaster was part of the habitual rhetoric of the idealist of the forlorn hope.[25]

Adams's images of drift, like Mark Twain's, were part of that rhetoric too. And so was a theory of history that, for all its impersonality, asserted the power of the human mind to absorb the vast forces impinging upon it.

How, according to Adams, do we know the tendency of history? Because of the unifying power of the individual mind: in the final phase of history, according to Adams's theory, all motion reached equilibrium in the universal solvent of pure thought, must as Theodor Fisher's universe resolved into "a *Thought*, a vagrant Thought" in *The Mysterious Stranger*.[26] Or much as past and present converged in the "roomy chambers" of Augustine's memory.[27] As Adams said of the universe in the chapter called "The Abyss of Ignorance": "One could know it only as one's self; it was psychology" (p. 432). Viewed in this light, the *Education* is the most egocentric of books, because, as Alfred Kazin has remarked, history to Henry Adams was his own consciousness of it.[28] From telling the story of a waif amid forces, the author of the *Education* had swung against the drift of his narrative to celebrate the mind of the lowly self as the sole instrument of measure in an otherwise fathomless multiverse. With this shift, Adams moved in the direction of his generation's major realignment in the writing of fiction.

In the mid-1880s, the realists had succeeded well enough at presenting the external lives of individual characters from limited narrative points of view to begin trying something else; by 1903, Howells observed in *Harper's* that a shift had indeed taken place: "A whole order of literature has arisen, calling itself psychological, as realism called itself scientific. . . . it is not less evident in Tolstoy, in Gorky, in Ibsen, in Björnsen, in Hauptmann, and in Mr. Henry James, than in Maeterlinck himself."[29] With *The Shadow of a Dream* (completed in 1889), Howells too had written a novel characterized by the increasingly *psychological* realism that in retrospect seems a likely sequel to the earlier realism's preoccupation with discrete individuals. After disclaiming narrative omniscience in order to see the world through the eyes of their characters, the realists accepted the next challenge and turned to see the reflected world in their characters' minds. They thus took on the responsibility Edith Wharton learned from James and declared to be the main business of the novelist in *The Writing of Fiction*: "not to ask what the situation would be likely to make of his characters, but what his characters, being what they are, would make of the situation."[30] When Adams held up his own consciousness as the only web in which history could be traced, the autobiographer's task merged with the "psychological" novelist's.

It is a seldom-noticed fact of American literary history that the movement of American fiction toward psychological modes in the 1890s and first decade of the new century coincided with the rise of modern autobiography in America. This phenomenon was anything but mere coincidence. When in 1889 Howells, for example, turned from writing *The Shadow of a Dream*, his first psychological novel, to begin and complete *A Boy's Town*, the first of his many autobiographical narratives, he was working in fundamentally the same medium. The autobiographer's greatest resource is memory, and to draw upon it Howells entered one of the larger chambers of the same haunted house that had been the province of proto-psychological fiction in America since Edgar Allan Poe. Moreover, as clearly intimated in *The Shadow of a Dream*, Howells and his contemporaries were on the brink of formulating a theory of the collective unconscious when they speculated that childhood recapitulated the primitive state of the human race. One need not declare them premature Jungians, therefore, to point out that Adams, Howells, Twain, and James recognized a close affinity between evoking one's remembered past and releasing the unconscious mind they were coming to recognize (and to resist) in their fiction. Certainly Adams's autobiography responded to the dangers they felt lurking beneath the surface of consciousness.

When he finished the *Education* in 1906, Adams still believed in the power of the conscious mind to devise a formula for its universe; but the book did not conceal signs that this belief would soon fail him. In the *Education*, history subsides into psychology, and psychology is yet another of Adams's rafts "to which the limpets stuck for life in the surge of a supersensual chaos" (p. 459). But this raft, like Huck Finn's, was precarious at best. Of all the force fields he ever studied, "pure thought" was to become the least attractive to one side of Adams's nature, though it comprised the only medium capable of holding his contraries in solution. Researches in contemporary psychology taught Adams to question the mind's power to integrate anything.

Marginal notes in his copy of William James's *Principles* indicate that the chief interest of the new science for Adams was its exploration of the submerged levels of consciousness; and in the *Education*, he reported the psychologists' findings as he understood them, "He gathered from the books that the psychologists had, in a few cases, distinguished several personalities in the same mind. . . . The new psychology went further, and seemed convinced that it had actually split personality not only into dualism, but also into complex groups, like telephonic centres and systems. . . . Alternating personalities turned up constantly, even among one's friends" (p. 433). Given such facts, Adams had to reason that the "only absolute truth" was "the sub-conscious chaos below" and that his sanity was just "unstable artifice": "He was an acrobat, with a dwarf on his back, crossing a chasm on a slackrope, and commonly breaking his neck" (pp. 433–34). One's own "consciousness" was itself chaotic; walking the paths of the newest science, Adams "saw no unity ahead—nothing but a dissolving mind" (434). Here was dissipation of a sort Saint Augustine had not contemplated.

By 1910, when he published *A Letter to American Teachers of History*, the work on which his undeserved reputation as a lifelong pessimist is based, Adams could see the mind only in this harsh light. In *A Letter*, the historian pondered the last enigma of his career: "If all the other sciences affirm that not Thought but Instinct is the potential of Vital Energy, and if the beauties of Thought—shown in the intuitions of artistic genius,—are to be taken for the last traces of an instinct now wholly dead or dying, nothing remains for the historian to describe or develop except the history of a more or less mechanical dissolution."[31] By defining thought as the dispersion of feeling and intuition, Adams discredited the one form of energy whose potential could be said to have increased in the twentieth century. With its halfhearted call for another Newton, *A Letter* showed that Adams's "search for the 'new mind' " had destroyed his confidence in the old mind without gaining him a compensating faith. Adams was referring to himself when he mentioned the dilemma of "the classical University teacher of history" caught between "two equilibriums, each mechanical, and each insisting that history is at an end."[32] To Adams in this state of mind, personal history served to illustrate only the impersonal nature of history in general. Looking back from the vantage of 1910, the *Education* could be interpreted not as the personal record of an ego swelling to encompass all recorded time but of an ego swallowed up in abstraction. For it could be seen to unveil a psychological determinism more troubling in its intimacy than the familiar determinism of historical and cultural forces. Seismic as always, Adams had touched upon perhaps the greatest perplexity that was occupying writers of fiction as they struggled to accommodate themselves to the unconscious. And by adopting a narrative form that attempted to trace its subject through the discrete phases of his life, Adams made his autobiography responsive to that related perplexity, illustrated acutely in the *Autobiography* of Mark Twain, of discovering continuity between an inescapably bewildering present and a seemingly idyllic past.

1. Worthington Chauncey Ford, ed., *Letters of Henry Adams*, vol. 2 (Boston and New York: Houghton Mifflin, 1938), p. 474. Ernest Samuels, ed., *The Education of Henry Adams* (Boston: Houghton Mifflin, 1973), p. 512. Ford, *Letters*, 2:542, 635.

2. Ford, *Letters*, 2:490, 477.

3. Ibid., p. 490.

4. *The Education of Henry Adams* (Boston and New York: Houghton Mifflin, 1918), p. vii. Copyright 1918 by the Massachusetts Historical Society; copyright 1946 by Charles F. Adams. Reprinted by permission of Houghton Mifflin Company. Subsequent references to the *Education* are to this edition and will appear in parentheses in the text.

5. Harold Dean Cater, ed., *Henry Adams and His Friends: A Collection of His Unpublished Letters* (Boston: Houghton Mifflin, 1947), p. 645.

6. Quoted in Ernest Samuels, *Henry Adams: The Major Phase* (Cambridge, Mass.: Harvard University Press, 1964), p. 313 (hereafter cited as *The Major Phase*).

7. Ernest Samuels, *The Young Henry Adams* (Cambridge, Mass.: Harvard University Press, 1948), pp. ix–x.

8. Samuels, *The Major Phase*, p. 313.

9. Ford, *Letters*, 2:70–71.

10. Ibid., p. 490. James, who took a case-study approach to religious experience, professed an "extraordinary longing" to read Adams's autobiography; autobiographies were his "particular line of literature, the only books I let myself buy outside of metaphysical treatises" (ibid., p. 485n).

11. Whitney J. Oates, ed., *Basic Writings of Saint Augustine* (New York: Random House, 1948), 1:20.

12. Ibid., p. 124.

13. Ibid., pp. 202, 214.

14. Ibid., p. 125.

15. J. C. Levenson, *The Mind and Art of Henry Adams* (Boston: Houghton Mifflin, 1957), p. 349.

16. *Basic Writings*, 1:196.

17. Brooks Adams, ed., *The Degradation of the Democratic Dogma* (New York: Macmillan, 1919), p. 276.

18. Ibid., pp. 267, 277.

19. Ibid., pp. 306, 308.

20. Ibid., p. 308.

21. Cater, *Adams and His Friends*, p. 645. Although the decline of allegorical personal narratives was one precondition of the rise of modern autobiography, Adams well knew the potential of allegory for creating drama. Bunyan made, he told Wendell, a "relative success" by using it; and Guillaume de Lorris achieved "the best popular triumph ever won" (ibid.). Both Adams and Saint Augustine had pushed beyond its limits an allegorical quest or journey form that works best when heaping up obstacles in the seeker's path but rapidly loses its dramatic potential when the goal is attained.

22. *Degradation*, pp. 308–9.

23. *Basic Writings*, 1:202.

24. Ford, *Letters*, 2:547.

25. *The Major Phase*, p. 362.

26. *Degradation*, p. 273. William M. Gibson, ed., *Mark Twain's Mysterious Stranger Manuscripts* (Berkeley and Los Angeles: University of California Press, 1969), p. 405.

27. *Basic Writings*, 1:152.

28. "History and Henry Adams," *New York Review of Books* 13 (October 1969): 28.

29. "Editor's Easy Chair," *Harper's Monthly Magazine* 107 (June 1903): 149.

30. (New York: Scribner's, 1925), p. 140.

31. *Degradation*, pp. 205–6.

32. Ibid., p. 249.

3

This Pathetic Drift
Mark Twain

> What a wee little part of a person's life are his acts
> and his words! His real life is led in his head, and is
> known to none but himself. All day long, and every
> day, the mill of his brain is grinding, and his *thoughts*,
> not those other things, are his history.—Samuel Clem-
> ens (ca. 1870)

Although Samuel Clemens and Henry Adams never met, the careers of the two men now seem to have run much closer together than Bernard DeVoto thought in 1940 when he labeled Adams "a Brahmin dilettante" as "unlike" Clemens "as possible."[1] Born within three years of each other, both spent the Civil War as secretaries to Lincoln appointees; both served literary apprenticeships as newspaper correspondents, almost crossing paths in Washington in 1868; both found the government "polluted with peculation"[2] and, in their thirties, attacked the crassness of the "gilded" age that was given its name by Clemens and Charles Dudley Warner. Habitual travelers who characterized themselves as innocents abroad, both men had difficulty settling down; but neither altogether escaped the puritanism that was no less Clemens's birthright for having come to him by way of Tennessee, Missouri, and Presbyterianism rather than Quincy, Harvard College, and the First Church of Boston. In later life, Adams and Clemens also suffered similar personal tragedies: Marian Adams's suicide and the sobering threat of bankruptcy at fifty-five may be placed beside Susy Clemens's fatal attack of meningitis, Olivia's invalidism, and the financial reverses that put Mark Twain back on the lecture platform at the age of sixty. And, of course, both came to contend with that malaise usually called "pessimism" in Adams's case and "despair" in Clemens's.

Less often but with no less justification, Clemens is also seen as flotsam weighted down on the unsteady currents of historiography by ideas similar to Adams's manikin's. As a general proposition, Clemens would have approved the underlying hypothesis that Adams's great *History of the United States* was written to test: that, in the history of this country, "war counted for little, the hero for less; on the people alone the eye could permanently rest."[3] The fictional editor of the "Eddypus" cycle attributed to its author an almost identical approach to American history: "His idea was that to write a minute history of persons, of all grades and callings, is the surest way to convey the intelligible history of the time; that it is not the illustrious only who illustrate history, all grades have a hand in it."[4] Concurring in the belief that common men rather than heroes provide the proper study of history in a democracy, Clemens also suffered Adams's loss of faith in eighteenth-century approaches to history. An avid reader of professional historians, the biographer of Joan of Arc began writing his "historical" fictions in the spirit of those eighteenth-century Whigs who thought the general lot of mankind was improving thanks to such legal and political advances as representative government, equality before the law, and the decline of royal privilege. Implicitly in *A Connecticut Yankee in King Arthur's Court* (1889) and overtly in *The American Claimant* (1892), however, Clemens revealed that he had lost confidence in history as a result of questioning man's moral superiority over his brute ancestors; and in *The Mysterious Stranger* he came to assert that the law of civilization was decay since moral corruption inhered in the race despite its veneer of culture.[5] Though he preferred cyclical metaphors, Clemens, like Adams, drifted from a positive belief in historical teleology to a negative vision of the degradation of democratic society. And though he regarded the Middle Ages as anything but a peak of civilization, Clemens had his own equivalent of the dynamo, that modern occult force to which Adams offered up a verse prayer. "You & I have imagined that *we* knew how to set type," he almost chanted in a letter inviting Howells to watch the Paige typesetter in operation. "Come & see the Master do it! Come & see this sublime magician of iron & steel work his enchantments."[6]

The man who hoped at one time to finish the Paige typesetter and *A Connecticut Yankee* on the same day suffered far more than financial losses when H. H. Rogers pronounced the typesetter a fiscal disaster. As with Adams, the machine failed Clemens as a substitute for divinity. The adoptive Yankee of Hartford, Connecticut, began his studies of history believing that technology could save mankind. When technology failed him, he was left with a view of history that seemed no longer reassuringly mechanistic but diabolically deterministic. Reduced to personal terms, historical determinism for Clemens came to resemble the psychological determinism that "soured" Adams in his very late writings. Clemens could not have known about Adams's concessions to psychological determinism in a letter to a fellow historian, Francis Parkman: "I am satisfied that the purely mechanical development of the human mind in society must appear in a great democracy so clearly, for want of disturbing elements, that in another generation psychology, physiology, and history will join in proving man to have as fixed and necessary development as that of a tree; and almost as unconscious."[7] But Clemens voiced similar ideas of his own concerning the newest science. "Man's proudest possession— his mind—" Clemens wrote in a gloss on *What Is Man?*, "is a mere machine: an automatic machine."[8] His copy of J. Mark Baldwin's *Story of the Mind* (1898) contained marginalia to the same effect. Where Baldwin asserted that the mind "grows" according to natural laws, Clemens wrote, "There is no mental *growth*. There is extension of mental *action*, but not of capacity." And to Baldwin's observation that "man himself is more of a machine than has been supposed," Clemens retorted: "He is wholly a machine."[9]

The tyranny of the machine and all it stood for had produced, Clemens felt, a race of displaced persons like Hank Morgan, that refugee from a lost Camelot who woke up in a bewildering present cut loose from all ties with the past. The similarities in their views of history came about in part because Adams and Clemens together belonged to the generation whose perception of history was altered by the national cataclysm that Henry James singled out in his biography of Hawthorne: "One may say that the Civil War marks an era in the history of the American mind. It introduced into the national consciousness a certain sense of proportion and relation, of the world being a more complicated place than it had hitherto seemed, the future more treacherous, success more difficult. . . ." The American of the future, James went on to say, would be a different person from his grandfather because he "has eaten of the tree of knowledge."[10]

James thus registered the sense of the past that was to distinguish his generation's response to history from that of Hawthorne's. Although James, like Hawthorne, later sought in Europe the antiquity he missed at home, many of James's contemporaries thought that America acquired a history and a past for the first time after the Civil War. (The highly developed historical sense of a Hawthorne or a Whittier had been fairly uncommon in a generation on the whole more taken with the all-encompassing Now of Emerson, Thoreau, and Whitman.) Yet America's "new" past, unlike that of Hawthorne's old Salem, seemed disinclined to lay its dead hand upon the present. Clemens, Adams, and Howells came increasingly to feel estranged from a past considerably enriched by their own nostalgic longings. Adams's belief that "the American boy of 1854

stood nearer the year 1 than to the year 1900" was shared by
many of the men who had scarcely emerged from adolescence
before being plunged into a civil war, who survived the war to
inaugurate Grant and industrial capitalism, and who then lived on to
enter the twentieth century well ahead of Europe, as Gertrude
Stein observed.[11] Victims or witnesses of this rapid national
aging process, many members of Clemens's generation came under the impression that their youth had been lost. This encoun-
ter with history brought psychic divisions of many kinds, for it
taught not only that postwar America was different from the
America they had been born into, but that they were different
people from themselves at an earlier date. To men who looked
back on a personal and national adolescence cut short by premature responsibility, the formative period between childhood
and adulthood took on a special importance.

What members of Clemens's generation often felt in retrospect was that they had had no real adolescence. When G.
Stanley Hall, for example, published his influential *Adolescence*
in 1904, he minimized the growing richness of the American
past by describing the county as "an unhistoric land"; but Hall
made the very scantiness of American history a factor governing
the adolescence of American youth. Since American customs,
literature, institutions, laws, and religion were inherited or imported "ready-made," he reasoned, American history enjoyed no
period of retardation in which these things could have developed
naturally; and by 1904, American life had sped up so enormous-
ly that the country was racing ahead of other nations in the
application of science and the development of new energy
sources for industry. Given this environment, Hall concluded,
"our young people leap rather than grow into maturity."[12]

Such conditions directly affected the writing of autobiography
in America. The education form was in part a response to those
theories of child development that held that the psyche grows
through a series of phases or stages; when, however, Adams,
Clemens, and their contemporaries examined their past lives in

memory, the connecting links between those stages seemed too often missing. To recollect one's personal history as a linear process of growing up posed the difficult challenge of discovering continuity in the lives of a generation that had all but bypassed adolescence in its rush toward a premature adulthood.

For Clemens, the challenge of connecting the world of the child with the world of the adult was especially acute. When he read part two of Howells's *Indian Summer* (1885), Clemens had been touched by this story of a foolish attempt to recover lost youth:

> It is a beautiful story, & makes a body laugh all the time, & cry inside, & feel so old & so forlorn; & gives him gracious glimpses of his lost youth that fill him with a measureless regret, & build up in him a cloudy sense of his having been a prince, once, in some enchanted far-off land, & of being in exile now, & desolate—& lord, no chance to ever get back there again! That is the thing that hurts.[13]

A Connecticut Yankee was in its early stages at the time Clemens wrote Howells; and within a few months, his notebook would mention a character of the nineteenth century who yearned for a lady left behind in Camelot.[14] The pleasurable anguish of this outpouring about an exiled prince in 1885 thus anticipated the unadulterated anguish of Hank Morgan's lament for the lost Sandy in 1889.

The challenge of history to run a thread of continuity between past and present was to defeat Clemens's narrative powers not only in *A Connecticut Yankee* but also in his inchoate *Autobiography*, begun soon after. Yet the mechanistic theory of history that caused Henry Adams to veer off into abstractions threatening the integrity of the individual mind caused Clemens, even when most divided from himself, to turn inward to the stream of his free-flowing consciousness for the only unity his discontinuous life story was to have. Instead of a search for method like the *Education of Henry Adams*, the *Autobiography* of Mark Twain was a revolt from method; it proceeded willy nilly because Clemens was trying desperately to escape the bitterness of Hank Morgan's tirade against "this plodding sad pilgrimage, this pathetic drift between the eternities."[15]

I

When Albert Bigelow Paine first broached the subject of an authorized biography in 1906, Clemens balked at "the idea of blocking out a consecutive series of events which have happened to me, or which I imagine have happened to me" (1:269).[16] Why this should be "impossible," Clemens did not say; but he had been thwarted by autobiographical forms often enough in the past to feel wary of the enterprise as Paine presented it. In both *Roughing It* (1872) and *Life on the Mississippi* (1883), Clemens had tried his hand at stories of education, and both books had broken down in the middle. Once Clemens's tender-foot learned to be Mark Twain and once his cub pilot became the realist for whom the language of the river conveyed natural facts no longer symbolic of spiritual facts, Clemens could go on writing only by switching narrative modes. Halfway through the two narratives he had given up personal history and reverted to the mode of the travel sketches, a form of diary writing— "news," Clemens called it—that reported on events roughly con-temporaneous with the moment of composition.

Clemens's chronic tendency to lose interest in long narratives may be adduced to explain these rifts. Moreover, by-the-pound subscription sales called for big books; so to pad out *Roughing It*, Clemens cannibalized his Sandwich Island and other dis-patches. And to more than double the size of "Old times on the Mississippi," he made the six weeks' journey that provided new material for contrasting the river in 1882 with the river of the late 1850s. But something more than the exigencies of publica-tion lies behind Clemens's difficulty with narratives of initiation and education. The *Autobiography* was not written for subscrip-tion, nor with the bulk of it did Clemens find the tank running dry as he often did in the middle of other long works. Yet that book is wrenched by the same divergent narrative impulses that pull apart Clemens's stories of education in the West and on the river. "It begins anywhere; it doesn't end at all; it has no skeleton and no adroit adjustment of members; it ranges through the Cosmos and arrives at Chaos," said a bewildered Brander Mathews in an early review of Paine's edition.[17] Side by side with recollections of Hannibal, obituaries of lost friends, and other evocations of his past, Clemens had placed portraits of living men, topical commentaries on current events, brief travelogues, and those snippets from newspapers, books, and letters that have prompted James M. Cox to describe the *Autobiography* as an example of the "extract" form.[18]

Seemingly unaware that he had concocted another American salmagundi, Clemens persisted in making virtues of the book's shortcomings. The "right way to do an Autobiography" had come to him, he said, while boarding with his dying wife at the Villa di Quarto in Florence in 1904: "Start it at no particular time of your life; wander at your free will all over your life; . . . drop it the moment its interest threatens to pale, and turn your talk upon the new and more interesting thing that has intruded itself into your mind meantime" (1:193). This discovery came simultaneously with Clemens's discovery of dictation. Always bonanza prone, he announced the find in a letter to W. D. Howells: "I've struck it! And I will give it away—to you. You will never know how much enjoyment you have lost until you get to dictating your autobiography; then you will realize, with a pang, that you might have been doing it all your life if you had only had the luck to think of it."[19] The structural chaos that Brander Mathews criticized in Clemens's *Autobiography* was traceable in part to the dictation method. Following the lure of effortless composition, Clemens launched himself upon a narrative that flowed "as flows the brook down through the hills and the leafy woodlands" (1:237). The result was what one might expect from a narrative that "*has no law*": it "never goes straight for a minute, but *goes*. . . . Nothing to do but make the trip; the how of it is not important, so that the trip is made" (1:237).

If by relying on dictation Clemens produced text without forcing himself to compose, his *Autobiography* further owed its lack of cohesion to a professed taste for diary writing and other forms of journalism on the part of the poor self-critic who once said he preferred the second half of *Roughing It* to the first.[20] In a chapter of *Life on the Mississippi* describing his stop at Vicksburg, Clemens had posed this conundrum: Why can a visitor who has only read about the great battle recount it more effectively than an eye witness? Because, he answered, long familiarity breeds boredom. To the man who makes a succession of voyages or lives through a protracted siege, "the thing has lost color, snap, surprise; and has become commonplace." Only limited exposure leaves a "deathless grip upon his imagination and memory."[21]

The *Autobiography* returned to this anomaly. He had first been impressed with the power of journalism, Clemens says, while preparing a magazine article in the fall of 1867. To find out the price of Indian corn in 1812, he had consulted a file of the *New York Evening Post* in the Library of Congress. Instead of statistics, Clemens found an absorbing account of the arrival of the British and the burning of the Capitol. Because the writer "delivered his words hot from the bat," his narrative made the reader's "blood leap fifty-nine years later" (1:325–26). Clemens got the same sense of immediacy from a special dispatch that appeared in the *New York Times* only a few days before he recalled the old newsletter. He reproduces the entire lengthy report of the "Morris incident" as a model of style because it is told in the language "we naturally use when we are talking about something that has just happened" (1:322). Such language makes diary writing much more compelling than history, says Clemens; it will last for "ages and ages" (1:322).

One of Clemens's unstated motives for writing about his life was to erect a personal monument or memorial that would last for ages and ages; and the very newness of news seemed to promise easy access to another Comstock Lode of enduring imaginative material. Instead of owning up to the book's defects, therefore, he pronounced it "a model for all future autobiographies" (2:245). By combining diary and autobiography, Clemens contended, he had invented "a form and method whereby the past and the present are constantly brought face to face, resulting in contrasts which newly fire up the interest all along like contact of flint with steel" (2:245). Clemens's form and method, however, did not so much solve his autobiographer's problems as reveal them. Admitting the wide difference between journalism and history, and between diary and autobiography, but claiming to believe "that news is history in its first and best form," Clemens tried to will the two into harmony (1:326). He began each morning's dictation "in diary form" and soon digressed from "the present text—the thought of to-day"—to wander "far and wide over an uncharted sea of recollection, and the result of that is *history*" (1:327). He had found a way, Clemens said, to write "diary and history combined" (1:328).

Surely this was a colossal rationalization. Some diaries, like Boswell's or Woolman's, show signs of considerable rewriting (as, for example, when incidents ostensibly recorded on one day clearly look forward to events of another that the diarist could have "anticipated" only in retrospect). All types of journal-keeping and journalism are strictly bound, however, merely to follow chronology on a day-by-day basis and are thus exempt from the demand of the education form to discover links between the days, years, and epochs of a life. If Clemens's *Autobiography* demonstrates anything, it demonstrates that "the dear and lamented past" and the "desolating future" were as irreconcilable for Clemens as news and history—the two major strands of his narrative (1:130; 2:314). "I can call it all back and make it as real as it ever was, and as blessed," the aging memorialist wrote in a set piece recalling his uncle's farm near Florida, Missouri (1:110). But the only tie with the past Clemens could be sure of in the *Autobiography* was the "decayed and rancid mush of inherited instincts and teachings derived, atom by atom, stench by stench," from the ancestral strain of moral corruption in the damned human race (2:9).

The *Autobiography* exposed a cherished lie: "to wit, that I am I, and you are you; that we are units, individuals, and have natures of our own" (2:9). Clemens's anti-form is best approached as a failed story of education in which the central figure imagines for himself no sequence of identities connecting the remembered world of boyhood with the far from idyllic world served up by his morning newspaper. The *Autobiography* betrayed once again the dilemma of a writer victimized by time as Hank Morgan is victimized in *A Connecticut Yankee*. The result for Clemens's narrative was the same debilitating clash in tone that mars the earlier work.

Almost any sequence in the *Autobiography* suffers from this clash, but the dictations of four days in March 1906 furnish an especially pointed example. During the first day, Clemens reminisces about life in Hannibal more than sixty years before. He recalls Tom Blankenship (model for Huck Finn), several classmates at Dawson's schoolhouse, and "that distant boy-Paradise, Cardiff Hill" (2:179). The dictations for the following day return to the subject of classmates, tracing several of them into later life. Then, in the last two passages of the series, Clemens's attention is diverted by a recent newspaper account of "the Moros Battle" in which American troops, led by General Wood, exterminated a tribe of "dark-skinned savages" as they huddled for protection in the crater of an extinct volcano (2: 187).

As the narrator of this sequence moves gradually from the distant past to the immediate present, he changes emotional perspective with each shift in time. At first, the tone is uniformly one of repose and idyllic calm. Even the death of Injun Joe holds no real terror for Clemens's remembered self. During the second day, however, a note of alarm enters Clemens's voice as he describes an old schoolmate: "*He died.* It is what I have to say about so many of those boys and girls" (2:184). And that voice grows shrill as the final dictations interpret the slaughter of the Moros with heavy irony: "The enemy numbered six hundred—including women and children—and we abolished them utterly, leaving not even a baby alive to cry for its dead mother. *This is incomparably the greatest victory that was ever achieved by the Christian soldiers of the United States*" (2:190).

Clemens's failure to reconcile the repose at the beginning of this sequence with the near-hysteria at the end indicates how the *Autobiography* typically falls apart, leaving the reader to connect Clemens's outbursts against present evils with his pastoral reminiscences of a far from pastoral childhood. Clemens supplies one conceivable link between his wildly variant moods, however, when he recalls watching a drunken tramp burn to death in a Hannibal jail cell. When hailed through the bars, young Clemens had supplied the tramp with matches and then had stood by helplessly as the man accidentally set himself on fire. For years afterward, the reproachful face of the dying man haunted Clemens's dreams. He was not morally responsible for the man's death, Clemens insists, because he meant the tramp no harm. But the boy could not escape his "trained Presbyterian conscience," which "knew but the one duty—to hunt and harry its slave upon all pretexts and on all occasions, particularly when there was no sense nor reason in it" (1:131).

Clemens's jeremiads upon the rancid human race owe their substance and spirit to the trained conscience that compelled Clemens (as it compelled Henry Adams) to measure life by absolute standards. When possessed by that conscience, which he once described as a grotesque dwarf, Clemens became the misanthropist of *What Is Man?*, and he became the autobiographer whose eruptions denounced government as a leech and humanity as a tapeworm. Yet it is tempting to accuse Clemens of excluding himself from his own indictment in the *Autobiography*. The book bears traces of that confessional literature which exposes sin not so much to seek punishment as to absolve the sinner by demonstrating that there can be "no sense nor reason" in punishing him. In laying the blame for man's failings upon innate depravity, Clemens retreated behind the poignant contradiction Justin Kaplan has seen in *What Is Man?*: "Without choice there can be no responsibility, and—as if Clemens dimly perceived the logical goal of his illogic—without responsibility guilt has no meaning."[22] As Bernard DeVoto once said, "No one, I think, can read this wearisomely repeated argument without feeling the terrible force of an inner cry: Do not blame me, for it was not my fault."[23] The *Autobiography* repeats Clemens's wearisome argument out of an obsessive need to establish his innocence in the debased present by showing himself to be the innocent child of a blessed past.

II

To leave the *Autobiography* on this note, however, would be to neglect the considerable degree of self-possession that Clemens actually achieved by assembling its chaotic mass. Clemens had no intention of writing the sort of autobiography he had promoted and published for General Grant. The "memoir" form was overly objective; his life story was to be a "mirror" turned upon himself rather than "an open window" through which the observer gazed at the passing scene (2:311-12). Dealing with a man's public words and deeds, the memoir ignored the "real life" he leads in his head: "All day long, and every day, the mill of his brain is grinding, and his *thoughts*, not those other things, are his history" (1:2).

Such history could not be written down, Clemens reluctantly conceded, because every day of one's life would require a whole book; and besides, the "volcanic fires" of our inner being lie buried too deep to be sounded (1:2). This is why biographies and autobiographies are "but the clothes and buttons of the man" (1:2). Yet Clemens's *Autobiography* revealed its author's inner consciousness in the way Howells divined in one of his keenest insights arising during his fifty years of devoted reading of Clemens's work. Having long noted the episodic freedom of his fiction, Howells observed in "Mark Twain: An Inquiry" (1901): "So far as I know Mr. Clemens is the first writer to use in extended writing the fashion we all use in thinking, and to set down the thing that comes into his mind without fear or favor of the thing that went before, or the thing that may be about to follow."[24] Clemens is seldom mentioned as a progenitor of the modern psychological novel, but if Clemens's characters were not so inner-directed as those of Henry James, few American authors before him so consistently left the imprint of their own mental processes upon the surface of their fiction. Writing rapidly, Clemens virtually translated the sequence of his thought into plot and style. Form followed method almost instantaneously. And though he did not "trace the threads of association" or pursue it by "design," free association was Clemens's basic method. Perhaps, as Howells said, he adopted it "from no wish but to have pleasure of his work, and not to fatigue either himself or his reader."[25]

When he dropped the pen to take up dictation in 1904, Clemens made the mind's unconscious method of association his conscious mode of narration. Moving like a "brook," his dictated *Autobiography* reflected the flow of Clemens's consciousness, and his lazy progress in talking himself out restored the joy of indolence and motion for its own sake that Clemens had conveyed in raft images before rafts in his fiction began drifting into ominous voids. Clemens's greatest difficulty with writing fiction had come about as he labored under a half-conviction in the mechanistic psychology that precipitated Hank Morgan's loss of humanity and that held special perils for the creative artist. In the *Autobiography*, Clemens professed still to believe in a mechanistic psychology; but by wandering at his "free will" over his life, he demonstrated that he also believed the operations of his consciousness to be more than the operations of an automaton. Pursuing the bent of his mind despite a theoretical commitment to determinism, Clemens trans-

formed the difficult act of writing his autobiography into a therapeutic exercise. In this, he resembled his friend Howells, whose
deeply disturbed psyche required corresponding therapy.

III

The fascination that children and childhood held for Clemens's
generation can be glimpsed nowhere more directly than in the
subspecies of autobiography they called "the boys' book." The
"bad" boys of Thomas Bailey Aldrich's *Story of a Bad Boy*
(1869), Charles Dudley Warner's *Being a Boy* (1878), and Howells's *A Boy's Town* (1890) bore little resemblance to the boys
in the romantic movement's literature of the child. They reveled
in a state of "savagery"—the normal condition of children, Hall's
Adolescence would remind parents years later—that was primitive
and innocent but seldom noble. Furthermore, they seemed infinitely far away. As late as 1855, Henry Wadsworth Longfellow's
poem, mistitled "My Lost Youth," achieved reunion of the mid-
dle-aged poet and the boy he had once been. When the authors
of the first American boy-books engaged in not so tranquil recollection, however, they seemed painfully conscious not only
that they and their boys looked out upon different worlds but
that they had come to see through utterly different eyes. The
vision of the child seemed lost beyond even fleeting recovery
to the adult. Thus a dominant tone in the boy-books was the
nostalgia informing this passage describing a child who dies in
Aldrich's *Story of a Bad Boy*:

> Poor little Binny Wallace! Always the same to me. The rest of us
> have grown up into hard, wordly men, fighting the fight of life; but
> you are forever young, and gentle, and pure; a part of my own
> childhood that time cannot wither; always a little boy, always poor
> little Binny Wallace![26]

It was probably such pathos as this that put Clemens off when
he first read *The Story of a Bad Boy* in 1869. "I could not admire
the volume much," he wrote Olivia in a Christmas note.[27]

Howells, however, could admire it, and his review for the *Atlantic* remarked Aldrich's "good fortune wherever he means to be pathetic." The chapter in which Binny Wallace died seemed to the reviewer "the best in the book." But Howells found more to admire in *The Story of a Bad Boy* than just the pathos arising from its glimpses of a lost Eden. The first boy-book appealed to his realist's temperament because it showed "what a boy's life is" instead of "teaching what it should be." Aldrich's narrative method was that of the autobiographer, Howells observed; and he predicted that it would some day produce that "pathetic antenatal phantom, pleading to be born into the world,—the American novel, namely."[28]

Howells's prediction was based on a revealing conflation of the boy-book, the novel, and the autobiography. Howells shrewdly perceived that Aldrich's originality lay in adapting the narrative techniques of autobiography to a story of childhood. The long-awaited American novel would come about when some gifted writer applied those same techniques "to more full-grown figures of fiction." There was thus in Howells's mind a close tie between fiction and the kind of "non-fictional" prose that charmed him above all others; so he was not much disturbed that Aldrich's story about Tom Bailey mixed "fact" and "feigning": "the author has the art which imbues all with the same quality, and will not let us tell one from the other." That art consisted in uniformly giving "his incidents and characters the simple order and air of actual occurrences and people."[29] Since this might well stand as a capsule statement of the realists' fictive creed, we would not be far off in defining the first modern autobiographies in America as narratives that combined the aims of realistic fiction with the narrative method of "the best and oldest masters of the art of story-telling."[30]

Indeed, Howells's prediction was not far wrong; for if the first boy-book led within a few years to *Tom Sawyer*, soon afterward a brilliant adaptation of the narrative techniques of auto-biography to a story of childhood produced the *Adventures of*

Huckleberry Finn, a book Clemens described to Howells in its early stages as both "another boys' book" and as "Huck Finn's Autobiography."[31] The new book revealed the typical problems with characterization that writers of Clemens's generation encountered because of inherent conflicts between the new theories of child development and the old theories they themselves had been brought up on; and it further revealed the peculiar difficulty Clemens had all his life with the education form.

Does Huck Finn mature? Readers who emphasize Huck's decision to go to hell rather than betray Jim down the river usually argue that Huck grows in some way. At first under the sway of Tom Sawyer and the values of the shore, he learns on the river to prize Jim's natural virtue; so schooled, he comes to pity even the Duke and the King when he sees them tarred and feathered ("Human beings can be awfully cruel to each other"); and he lights out for the Indian territory at the end of the novel rather than return to a "civilization" he has risen above morally. Interpreted thus, Huck's history is an old-fashioned story of cultivation based on the head-heart psychology underlying the fiction, say, of Hawthorne. Huck's conscience—an essentially cognitive faculty shaped by social norms—has become overdeveloped thanks to his upbringing by the Widow Douglas and that ultimate conformist, Pap. The experience with Jim on the raft, however, provides vital nourishment for Huck's sound but previously stunted heart, enabling the boy to combat his deformed conscience and expand to his true moral stature.

Readers who emphasize the closing chapters of Huck's history, on the other hand, often argue that Huck does not develop systematically or even coherently. The episodes at the Phelps plantation end with Huck back where he started—as the boy-book pal of Tom Sawyer. Huck once in a while objects to Tom's handling of Jim's escape, all right; but he is no different from the Huck at the beginning of the novel who said Tom's caravan of A-rabs had all the marks of a Sunday School party. Conversely, the man-child who right away figures the Duke and the King for confidence men seems to bear little resemblance to the innocent who is later fooled by the "drunken" bareback rider at the circus. According to this interpretation, Huck's character depends largely upon circumstance; its only constant is that Huck prefers to take the easy way out of any predicament.

Debate over Clemens's characterization of Huck is likely to go on indefinitely because the novel yields evidence on both sides; building upon potentially conflicting psychologies, Clemens's fiction unwittingly mirrored the conflict. Yet Clemens might have achieved a closer harmony between the two than he did. If *Huckleberry Finn* attests the situational nature of character; it seems little touched by any notion of predictable stages in the history of the psyche's interplay with circumstance. (Hence the difficulty of pinning down Huck's age, which seems to waiver between twelve and fourteen or between eight and eighty.) The new psychology said that consciousness is a stream whose particles are always changing; yet it also said that those particles formed part of a continuum. Had Clemens discerned continuity in Huck's responses to his adventures as he drifted down the river, he might have made Huck's education reinforce the cultivation of his good heart. Here, however, was the shoal where Clemens's narratives of education usually foundered.

When Clemens wrote Howells that he had finished *Tom Sawyer*, he said he had not taken his hero past boyhood. Some day he would run a boy of twelve on through to manhood, and he would do it in the first person. But Tom was not the character for such a narrative, Clemens said; if his history were continued, he would end up just like all the other "one-horse men in literature."[32] When Clemens got around to writing Huck Finn's autobiography, he carried out his plan for a first-person narrative point of view; why he did not follow through on the other part of his plan can only be conjectured. But the evidence of *Mark Twain's Autobiography* suggests that Clemens feared all boys turned into merely "one-horse" men when they left the charmed circle of boyhood. By sending Huck Finn to the territory,

Clemens kept Huck from growing up; and he temporarily kept himself from having to face the mystery of adolescence, a region stretching toward Eden on one side and the Gilded Age on the other. In his *Autobiography*, Clemens still had not penetrated that mystery; the division seemed wider than ever.

1. *Mark Twain in Eruption: Hitherto Unpublished Pages about Men and Events* (New York: Harper, 1940), p. xxviii.
2. Louis J. Budd, *Mark Twain: Social Philosopher* (Bloomington: Indiana University Press, 1962), p. 35.
3. Vol. 9 (New York: Scribner's, 1891), p. 224.
4. Quoted in Roger B. Salomon, *Twain and the Image of History* (New Haven: Yale University Press, 1961), p. 21.
5. The progress of Clemens's disenchantment with "the Whig hypothesis" in these three books is charted in ibid., pp. 3–32. For Clemens's debt to eighteenth-century historians and the Jeffersonian tradition, see also Henry Nash Smith, *Mark Twain: The Development of a Writer* (Cambridge, Mass.: Harvard University Press, 1962), pp. 152–53.
6. Henry Nash Smith and William M. Gibson, eds., *Mark Twain-Howells Letters: The Correspondence of Samuel L. Clemens and William D. Howells, 1872–1910* (Cambridge, Mass.: Harvard University Press, 1960), p. 615.
7. Harold Dean Cater, ed., *Henry Adams and His Friends* (Boston: Houghton Mifflin, 1947), p. 134.
8. Quoted in Justin Kaplan, *Mr. Clemens and Mark Twain: A Biography* (New York: Simon & Schuster, 1966), p. 340.
9. Quoted in Albert E. Stone, Jr., *The Innocent Eye: Childhood in Mark Twain's Imagination* (New Haven: Yale University Press, 1961), p. 241.
10. *Hawthorne* (New York: Harper & Bros., 1879), pp. 139–40.
11. *The Education of Henry Adams* (Boston and New York: Houghton Mifflin, 1918), p. 53. America, said Gertrude Stein, is "the oldest country in the world" because her lead in industrial technology brought her "into the twentieth century in the eighties before any other country had any idea what the twentieth century was going to be" (Carl Van Vechten, ed., *Selected Writings of Gertrude Stein* [New York: Random House, 1946], p. 621).
12. *Adolescence* (New York: Appleton, 1904), p. xvi. The impact of child psychology upon American literature is assessed in Jay Martin, *Harvests of Change: American Literature, 1865–1914* (Englewood Cliffs, N.J.: Prentice-Hall, 1967), pp. 81–88.
13. Smith and Gibson, *Mark Twain-Howells Letters*, pp. 533–34.

14. Henry Nash Smith cites Clemens's notebook number 20 (Aug. 1885–Jan. 1886) in *Mark Twain's Fable of Progress: Political and Economic Ideas in "A Connecticut Yankee"* (New Brunswick, N.J.: Rutgers University Press, 1964), p. 43.

15. *A Connecticut Yankee in King Arthur's Court* (New York: Charles L. Webster, 1889), p. 217.

16. Clemens's story of his life exists in no authoritative final form but sprawls over hundreds of manuscript pages among the Mark Twain Papers, now being edited at Berkeley. Portions of the autobiographical dictations were published in the *North American Review* from September 1906 to December 1907 and in *Harper's*, February, March, and August 1922. With some additions and deletions, this material was collected by Albert Bigelow Paine in two volumes, *Mark Twain's Autobiography* (New York: Harper, 1924). Bernard DeVoto brought out approximately half of the remaining manuscript material in *Mark Twain in Eruption* (New York: Harper, 1940); and Charles Neider estimated that he was adding another 30,000 to 40,000 words in *The Autobiography of Mark Twain: Including Chapters Now Published for the First Time* (New York: Harper & Row, 1959). The Paine edition is cited here in parentheses in the text.

17. Quoted in Neider, *The Autobiography of Mark Twain*, p. xvii.

18. *Mark Twain: The Fate of Humor* (Princeton, N.J.: Princeton University Press, 1966), p. 305.

19. Smith and Gibson, *Mark Twain-Howells Letters*, p. 778.

20. When he had finished about two-thirds of *Roughing It*, Clemens wrote Elisha Bliss: "I am not half as well satisfied with the first part of the book as I am with what I am writing now" (*Mark Twain's Letters*, ed. Albert Bigelow Paine [New York and London: Harper, 1917], p. 187).

21. *Life on the Mississippi* (Boston: Osgood, 1883), p. 379.

22. *Mr. Clemens and Mark Twain*, p. 340.

23. *Mark Twain at Work* (Cambridge, Mass.: Harvard University Press, 1942), p. 116. In *Mark Twain in Eruption*, p. xviii, DeVoto focused on the "anxiety, violence, supernatural horror, and . . . enveloping dread" of Clemens's recollections of boyhood. His "Symbols of Despair" essay, however, said that boyhood was Clemens's "golden time and that Hannibal was his lost, immortal idyll, not of boyhood only but of home as well" (*Mark Twain at Work*, p. 115). Clearly, in Clemens's recollection, boyhood represented both.

24. *North American Review* 531 (February 1901): 307. Howells repeated his assessment in *My Mark Twain* (1910): ". . . He wrote as he thought, and as all men think, without sequence, without an eye to what went before or should come after. . . . He observed this manner in the construction of his sentences, and the arrangement of his chapters, and the ordering or disordering of his compilations" (David F. Hiatt and Edwin H. Cady, eds., *Literary Friends and Acquaintance* [Bloomington: Indiana University Press, 1968], p. 266).

25. "Mark Twain: An Inquiry," p. 308.

26. *The Story of a Bad Boy* (Boston: Houghton Mifflin, 1877), pp. 163–64. Aldrich's boy-book was first published in 1869.

27. Dixon Wecter, *The Love Letters of Mark Twain* (New York: Harper, 1949), p. 132.

28. *Atlantic Monthly* 25 (January 1870): 124–25.

29. Ibid., p. 124.

30. Ibid., p. 124.

31. Smith and Gibson, *Mark Twain-Howells Letters*, p. 144.

32. Ibid., p. 91.

4

The Wilderness Within
W. D. Howells

> Nearly all the lines of his figure are curved. His hands are fat and dimpled. His round face has the look of refinement, experience of the world, the good-natured indifference and the cynically happy disbelief of a diplomat of experience and high position. . . . There are certain notes of contentment in the tone of his voice which argue that Mr. Howells is satisfied with his career and with the success he has made in life.—T. C. Crawford (1892)

> How gladly I would never speak of myself again! But it's somehow always being tormented out of me, in spite of the small pleasure and pride the past gives me. "It's so damned humiliating," as Mark Twain once said of *his* past.—W. D. Howells to Thomas Bailey Aldrich (1900)

In March 1910, *Harper's Bazar* carried an autobiographical essay by W. D. Howells that might lead unwary modern readers to expect a success story whenever the venerable "dean" of American letters recounted episodes in his personal history. "The Turning Point of My Life" recalled the day, almost fifty years before, when Howells learned that the *North American Review* would publish his essay "Recent Italian Comedy." Editor James Russell Lowell's offer of generous access to the *Review* seemed to bear out Dr. Holmes's witty prophecy that Howells stood in direct "apostolic succession" to the New England literati.[1] It was with a due sense of proportion, then, that Howells in

1910 recalled Lowell's gracious letter of acceptance as a high-water mark in his career. Yet the novelist who was first among his contemporaries to study profoundly the mind of the business-man in fiction had his doubts about "turning points" as popu-larly conceived. By contributing to a series of autobiographical essays commissioned expressly in the success story mode, Howells had been obliged to conform his life to a salient feature of that literature in which finding a wallet or rescuing a rich man's daughter boosts the worthy hero to the first rung of the ladder. The turning-point essay in *Harper's Bazar*, however, was uncharacteristic of the writer who turned the conventions of the success story upside down in the history of that solid man of Boston, Silas Lapham. For Howells, the rising action of Silas's fictional career could not occur until the usual direction of the business hero's fortunes had been reversed. Instead of regard-ing the successful businessman as the highest product of social evolution, Howells's economic novels (more "socialistic" by far than John Hay's *The Breadwinners*, Henry Adams's *Democracy*, or even the essentially jingoistic *Connecticut Yankee*) portrayed him as a moral nonentity. In the words of the aging Bromfield Corey of *The Quality of Mercy*, Howells believed that the com-mercial rise of a Lapham or a Dryfoos or a Northwick was "preceded by the slow and long decay of a moral nature."[2] This was why, like the biblical Jacob to whom he often com-pares them, Howells's proud businessmen had to be humbled before they could begin to be morally strengthened.

Howells was fascinated with the business mind for reasons almost directly opposed to those that made tycoon-worshipers of many Americans in the 1870s and 1880s. A prosperous mas-ter of the art of renegotiating contracts, Howells was himself a shrewd man of affairs. But young Howells had loved Long-fellow's Cambridge for its vestiges of village culture in which money seemed to count for little; New York remained for him a commercial rather than a literary capital—when he could bring himself to call it a capital at all. There was more of the socialist than the financial aristocrat in the man who denounced an American plutocracy before Mark Twain did, whose greatest literary passion was Tolstoy, and who came to believe that America would have a better democracy when it had economic equality. Furthermore, Bromfield Corey's remark that money had become the romance and poetry of late nineteenth-century America rang true enough to arouse a realist's combative instincts.[3] Aiming at false idealizations of all kinds in literature, Howells did not overlook those romances of the business life which proclaimed that the right lucky break, combined with pluck and virtue, inexorably brought respectability and a pot of gold. To the mature Howells, culture heroes who were supposed to advance relentlessly upward in unbroken curves from fixed turning points were as unrealistic as those characters of romance who (he charged in *Criticism and Fiction*) display scant "living growth, but are apt to be types, limited to the expression of one principle, simple, elemental, lacking the God-given complexity of motive which we find in all the human beings we know."[4]

Defining the apparently rising action of the conventional success story as a moral decline and fall, Howells was not likely to adopt the success story model for his own autobiography. Besides, his culture's clichés about the businessman did not comport with the principles of character formation inculcated in him since childhood. The mature Howells, it is true, could not accept the philosophical idealism inherent in his father's Swedenborgian teachings. William Cooper Howells's faith in a direct correspondence between natural and spiritual facts eluded his son as it eluded the son of another remarkable Swedenborgian, Henry James, Jr. But if Howells rejected his father's metaphysics, vestiges of the elder Howells's Swedenborgian psychology stayed with the son to color his understanding of the mechanisms of self-definition.

Not surprisingly, Basil March's theory of character formation in *A Hazard of New Fortunes*—"There's the making of several characters in each of us; . . . and sometimes this character has the lead in us, and sometimes that"—reappears but slightly altered in many of Howells's other works.[5] "We all have twenty different characters," says Mrs. Brinkley of *April Hopes*, "and we put them on and take them off . . . for different occasions."[6] Likewise, the paternal narrator of *A Boy's Town* tells his young readers, "Every boy is two or three boys, or twenty or thirty different kinds of boys in one; he is all the time living many lives and forming many characters; but it is a good thing if he can keep one life and one character when he gets to be a man."[7] And of the two passages Howells the reviewer selected for extended quotation in his notice of *The Principles of Psychology*, one summarized James's theory of consciousness as an ever changing stream: "Every thought we have of a given fact . . . is, strictly speaking, unique. . . . When the identical fact recurs, we *must* think of it in a fresh manner, see it under a somewhat different angle, apprehend it in different relations from those in which it last appeared. . . . Often we are ourselves struck at the strange differences in our successive views of the same thing."[8]

Swedenborg's description of personality as a set of contending agents had prepared Howells to apprehend the self as a multiple rather than a unit, the key innovation of modern over "classic" psychology according to William James. Yet Howells was as reluctant as James to rely upon a "contingent" psychology for evading the responsibility of defining his own identity. From William Cooper Howells he had learned that "a man's love was his very self," and it would have gone against this fundamental precept to say flatly that one possessed no stable character, because character inevitably changed with circumstance.[9] Thus, though Howells asserted that character is multiple, he also asserted (in accordance with another major tenet of Swedenborg's psychology) that character tends to solidify over a long period of time. After observing how we put different characters on and off, Mrs. Brinkley of *April Hopes* wonders about the fate of the book's heroine, Alice Pasmer. "It isn't what she is now, or seems to be, or thinks she is. It's what she's going to finally harden into—what's going to be her prevailing character."[10]

Howells's editorial comments in his review of James's *Principles* put responsibility for one's "prevailing character" squarely upon the self. Noting that "we are creatures of our own making," Howells concluded in explicitly Swedenborgian terms: "It is this preference [either for virtue or vice] which at last becomes the man, and remains permanent throughout those astounding changes which every one finds in himself from time to time."[11] Prompted by a Swedenborgian tendency to find proof of moral freedom in habitual conduct, Howells read James's chapter on the will in the light of his chapter on habit; and he used James's observations to support a contention worthy not only of Swedenborg but of Saint Augustine. "In fact," Howells wrote, "the will of the weak man is *not* free; but the will of the strong man, the man who has *got the habit* of preferring sense to nonsense and 'virtue' to 'vice,' is a *freed* will. . . ."[12]

Howells's autobiographical writings of the period, however, shed doubt on this comforting conclusion. The most pressing of all Howells's reasons for rejecting the success story model was that even his immediate past held too many rough spots to be easily assimilated into a self-congratulatory chronicle of smooth ascent. Beginning in October 1885, when his daughter Winifred's evasive illness dramatically recurred, Howells had been beset with a series of domestic tragedies. Little more than a year later, he reached Jefferson, Ohio, in time to see malaria kill the sister who had shared his boyhood devotion to literature. And in March 1888, Elinor Howells declined into a lasting neurasthenia similar to the more celebrated invalidism of her friend Olivia Clemens. Still more harrowing, Winifred Howells died in March 1889 while under the specialist's care of S. Weir Mitchell, America's leading pre-Freudian alienist, who believed with other physicians that her malady was psychosomatic. When it was determined after Winifred's death that the disease in fact stemmed from physical causes, Howells blamed himself for carrying out the doctors' regimen of force-feeding and enforced cheerfulness.

The psychic pressures and guilt feelings of his "black time" drove Howells to overcome the reluctance he had always felt about reviewing his childhood and youth.[13] The return to his personal past that began with *A Boy's Town* (1890) was prolonged through *My Year in a Log Cabin* (1893), *My Literary Passions* (1895), and *Impressions and Experiences* (1896). Howells had just finished *Literary Friends and Acquaintance* when he confided to Thomas Bailey Aldrich in 1900 that the past gave him "small pleasure and pride" even though it was constantly being "tormented" out of him: " 'It's so damned humiliating,' as Mark Twain once said of *his* past."[14]

Although Howells's autobiographical volumes hold no hope of returning to the lost innocence of boyhood, they indicate that certain aspects of a disturbed past remained all too accessible to Howells in later years, and they further indicate that reminiscence tormented Howells for the very reasons Clemens found liberating. Because growing up (and therefore growing further away from a troubled childhood) had restored Howells to psychic health, his autobiographical writings betray none of Clemens's difficulties in passing from one stage of development to another. *A Boy's Town* is an apparently confident story of education along conventional lines: but though it follows the education model, it also follows the intriguing advice that Howells gave to would-be autobiographers many years later in *Years of My Youth*, a narrative that was more open with Howells's readers and with himself:

> Let him not be afraid of being too unsparing in his memories; the instinct of self-preservation will safeguard him from showing himself quite as he was. No man, unless he puts on the mask of fiction, can show his real face or the will behind it. For this reason the only real biographies are the novels, and every novel, if it is honest, will be the autobiography of the author and biography of the reader.[15]

Begun when the instinct of self-preservation had been re-kindled in Howells by the recent traumas in his private life, *A Boy's Town* spared no efforts to erect safeguards that would shelter and conceal a threatened psyche. Yet Howells was tormented all the more when reminiscence turned up little evidence of psychological free will. Evoking his past at the same time that he was discovering the unconscious mind as a tangled field of exploration in fiction, Howells met in his remembered childhood and youth the same threatening, sometimes terrifying, disorder and lack of restraint he was coming to associate with the unconscious. Like Clemens, Howells knew that without responsibility guilt has no meaning; but burdened from childhood with a sense of duty to define himself in ethical relation to others, he also felt that without responsibility there could be no moral or personal fulfillment. Such are the submerged complexities of *A Boy's Town*, the best of Howells's autobiographical volumes and a book that has never been adequately examined in its own right.

I

As if in anticipation of Freud's later study of the unconscious mind as it emerges both through memory and in dreams, Howells came to write *A Boy's Town* immediately after completing the first of his psychological novels, *The Shadow of a Dream* (1890). Though almost contemporaneous, the two books are usually treated as divergent narratives; they are, however, much more closely related than is generally supposed. Because the novel is virtually an introduction to its autobiographical sequel, a proper study of *A Boy's Town* starts there. In *The Shadow of a Dream*, the doomed midwesterner Douglas Faulkner is the victim of an obsessive nightmare in which he sees his own funeral merge with the hasty marriage of his wife, Hermia, and his best friend, the Reverend James Nevil. Faulkner interprets the dream as inspired prophecy, willfully rejecting a theory of the sleeping mind that might have borrowed its key metaphor

from William James: "There's a whole region of experience—
half the map of our life—that they tell us must always remain a
wilderness, with all its extraordinary phenomena irredeemably
savage and senseless."[16] Faulkner is not alone in shunning the
theory that the mind has dark fringes beyond its sunlit terrace.
Basil and Isabel March hesitate to credit the notion of an unconscious mind, and Isabel will not permit it "to be said, or
even suggested, that our feelings are not at our bidding, and
that there is no sin where there has been no sinning" (p. 115).
Only Nevil and Hermia come to believe, after Faulkner's death,
that they loved "unknowingly" (p. 107). Stricken with guilt,
they give each other up, and Nevil is killed by a train an instant
after he promises March to return to Hermia.

Philosophically and morally, the minister's scruples appear
seriously misplaced, for if he and Hermia are innocent of adul-
terous acts or even intentions, as the Marches think, why must
they endure the suffering of the guilty? A partial answer is
Howells's familiar doctrine of "complicity," which comforts
even James Nevil: "No pang we suffer in soul or sense is lost
or wasted, but is suffered to the good of some one, or of all.
How, we shall some time know; and why. For the present the
assurance that it is so, is enough for me . . . " (pp. 24–25).
March agrees, and he offers a new rationale for believing in
human complicity to go with Howells's usual one of spiritual
need: "Was existence all a miserable chance, a series of stupid,
blundering accidents? We could not believe that, for our very
souls' sake; and for our own sanity we must not" (p. 59).

To Howells a few months after the long trauma of Winifred's
malady had ended for her but not for her parents, March's second reason for discerning purpose behind the mystery of human
suffering must have had a special force, and it is easy (though
finally erroneous) to identify Howells with the sturdy character
who sometimes voices his ideas in other novels. When, for example, March accompanies Hermia on the long train ride to
Faulkner's family home, he not only returns to a midwestern

city resembling the Columbus, Ohio, of Howells's own youth, he also crosses the frontiers of his personal past just as Howells was to do almost before *The Shadow of a Dream* was finished. March further resembles Howells in contemning the "infernal juggle of the morbid conscience" by which Nevil tells himself that he desperately sinned (p. 111). Howells's autobiographical writings reveal that he too suffered the pangs of a morbid conscience and that he often despaired of bringing them into balance with the dictates of his rational mind. And surely we are expected to see the author of *A Boy's Town* in the fictional character who finds Faulkner "uncivilized" and who will not believe in Faulkner's dream as prophecy because he steadfastly refuses to "return to the bondage of the superstitions that cursed the childhood of the race, that blackened every joy of its youth and spread a veil of innocent blood between it and the skies" (p. 32).

But Howells and March part company when March refuses to believe in Faulkner's dream as a valid reflection of man's inner consciousness. If Howells was finally able to escape morbid introspection and take himself outside the depths of his troubled psyche, as March says James Nevil should, Howells knew too well the real shadows that dream-thoughts can project across our waking lives to condone March's dismissal of the irrational in human behavior. The issue in *The Shadow of a Dream* is not whether the dream had substance; whether Nevil and Hermia actually committed unconscious adultery is almost irrelevant. It is the question of control raised by the wilderness metaphor that Howells gives Faulkner to reject. That it cannot be rejected is suggested by Howells's description of the ruined garden in which Faulkner dies:

> Within the garden close there were old greenhouses and graperies, their roofs sunken in and their glass shattered, where every spring the tall weeds sprang up to the light, and withered in midsummer for want of moisture, and the Black Hamburgs and Sweetwaters set in large clusters whose berries mildewed and burst, and mouldered away in never-riping decay. Broken flower-pots strewed the ground

about them, and filled the tangles of the grass; but nature took up the work from art, and continued the old garden in her wilding fashion. . . . Neglected rose-bushes straggled and fell in the high grass, their leaves tattered and skeletoned by slugs and blight; but here and there they still lifted a belated flower. The terraced garden beds were dense with witch-grass, through which the blackberry vines trailed their leaves, already on fire with autumn; young sumach-trees and Balm of Gilead scrub had sprung up in the paths, and about among the abandon and oblivion of former symmetry, stiff borders of box gave out their pungent odor in the sun that shone through clumps of tiger-lilies. (Pp. 26–27)

Though March does not realize it, this ruined garden serves both as a metaphor for Faulkner's disordered mind and as an objectification of the depths of March's own psyche. This is why Howells has March say, a page later, that a landscape he has never seen before is "as familiar to me as any most intimate experience of my life" (p. 28). And like the "seasonless, changeless, boundless" ocean that it overlooks, Faulkner's garden is characterized primarily by its wildness and freedom from normal limits and boundaries (p. 35).

Howells was later to force a tenuous balance between free will and psychological fatalism by reasoning that we are responsible for our conscious acts even though we cannot control our unconscious desires. "There is no sin where there has been no sinning," he inscribed inside a copy of *The Shadow of a Dream* in April 1905.[17] But in 1890, Howells (unlike March, who condones Isabel's imperious dismissal of the unconscious) could not so placidly neutralize the dark influence of the sleeping mind. Bereaved and bewildered by recent events in his personal life, Howells was primed for the unsettling knowledge that the unconscious opens the way to primitive states of being: the unconscious appeared as a repository of "the powers of darkness that work upon our nerves through the superstitions of the childhood of the world" (p. 112). To come under the control of the unconscious mind was to revert to childhood, an estate that held for Howells no memories of vanished glory. Both the unconscious mind and the mind of the child appeared to him savage and senseless, and it was in the discovery and exploration of their common wildness that Howells's impulse to write psychological fiction had its common origin with the impulse to cast up in memory the substantial shadows of his own childhood dreams and presentiments.

II

A Boy's Town shows conclusively that the past's humiliating influence went back beyond the tragedies of Howells's black time to the earliest impressions he could remember.[18] Interwoven with its pleasant anecdotes and its generalities about boy-life and smoothed over by a reassuring, genial tone, there are scattered recollections of neurotic tendencies that might well have debilitated a weaker nature without Howells's compensating resources. Howells remembers, for instance, that he "early heard of forebodings and presentiments, and he tried hard against his will to have them, because he was so afraid of having them."[19] A similar imp of the perverse caused him to envision his own funeral and see himself just saved from being buried alive by someone's realizing that he was only in a trance. He was terrified of dying, and when he started creating simple fictions, he grew afraid, if he imagined a character's death, that he was that character and would soon die. When doomsayers in the town announced the end of the world, young Howells "took the tint of the prevailing gloom" (p. 203). And when he was shown a picture of death on a pale horse, his soul was "harrowed" by its "ghastliness" (p. 216). The town crazy man, Solomon Whistler, "froze his blood and shrivelled him up with terror" (p. 25). The sight of a knot of spring snakes in a cornfield reappeared to haunt his dreams, and he ran by the stonecutter's yard in broad daylight for fear of ghosts (p. 200). In short, Howells confesses, "he dwelt in a world of terrors" (p. 56). Little wonder then that *Years of My Youth* mentions "the fear which is the prevailing mood of childhood."[20]

The anxieties that caused Dr. S. Weir Mitchell to "shiver" with interest when he read *A Boy's Town* came slowly to focus in a single delusion, reported there in chilly detail:[21]

> Once, he woke up in the night and found the full moon shining into his room in a very strange and phantasmal way, and washing the floor with its pale light, and somehow it came into his mind that he was going to die when he was sixteen years old. He could then only have been nine or ten, but the perverse fear sank deep into his soul, and became an increasing torture till he passed his sixteenth birthday and entered upon the year in which he had appointed himself to die. (P. 204)

Here is Hawthorne's neutral territory transformed into a region of psychological terror, and it may be that Howells's preference for the common daylight of realism over the moonlight of romance owed a great deal to his early knowledge of the havoc that moon-bathed fantasies can produce in some hypersensitive minds. At any rate, Howells was anxious to ease his morbid recollection with a realist's humor, the defense mechanism he relied on almost as often as Mark Twain did. When he turned sixteen, Howells recalls, the "agony was then too great for him to bear alone any longer," and he confessed it to his sympathetic father (p. 204). " 'Why,' his father said, 'you are in your seventeenth year now. It is too late for you to die at sixteen' " (p. 204). With this rejoinder, supposedly, the boy's burden of misery lifted and he recovered. "If he had known that he would be in his seventeenth year as soon as he was sixteen," says the memorialist, "he might have arranged his presentiment differently" (p. 204).

But that presentiment was not taken lightly either at the time it occurred or at the time Howells recounted it. The specific agent of Howells's self-appointed doom was rabies (or "hydrophobia"); and in the summer of either 1854 or 1856, young Howells induced in himself the symptoms of the disease.[22] The sound of running water, he said in *Years of My Youth*, almost sent him into convulsions, and the smell of forest fires outside the village became "the subjective odor of smoke which stifles the victim."[23] For a time, his obsession did not abate "except in the dreamless sleep which I fell into exhausted at night, or that little instant of waking in the morning, when I had not yet had time to gather my terrors about me, or to begin the frenzied stress of my effort to experience the thing I dreaded."[24]

It is essential for even the haziest understanding of the state of mind that produced *A Boy's Town* to appreciate the differences between Howells's presentation of his "hypochondria" in 1890 and in 1916, when he published the patchwork volume, *Years of My Youth*. The narrator of *A Boy's Town* typically neutralizes disturbing memories either by hinting that they fall within the general fantasies and superstitions of all boys or by airing them in the warmth of his sunny disposition. When "something dreadful happens," the narrator is able to say, it later seems "not to have happened; but a lovely experience leaves a sense of enduring fact behind, and remains a rich possession no matter how slight and simple it was" (pp. 18-19). Despite all the waterways in the book, the narrator of *A Boy's Town* does not mention death by rabies, or the revulsion to water that accompanies the disease, except when he alludes offhandedly to the "dreadful afternoon" his boy spent cowering in the woodshed with the family dog. (For no good reason, Howells had convinced himself that the dog was going mad.) In *Years of My Youth*, however, Howells's childhood dread of rabies is a central event. And although in 1916 he still could not write the word *hydrophobia* without a "shutting of the heart," Howells openly recorded his neurosis, he said, because "I think it essential to the study of my very morbid boyhood."[25]

Howells's understanding of how he came to conquer his neurosis is a matter of record. Long walks and other exercise to the point of exhaustion helped, as did his father's patience and advice. Also, Howells learned from a friendly doctor to treat his hypochondria lightly as "my hippo."[26] Taken together, such remedies taught him the "psychological juggle" (of the "morbid conscience," Basil March might have added) that he describes in *Years of My Youth*: "I came to deal with my own state of mind as another would deal with it, and to combat my fears as if they were alien."[27]

The ploy of holding himself at arm's length by using the third person indicates that Howells was still practicing his juggle when he wrote *A Boy's Town*. From the opening paragraph, the book is distinguished by the voice of a genial narrator who refers to his youthful self in the third person as "my boy" (p. 2). Except that he speaks to an audience composed largely of children and adolescents, this venerable figure resembles the persona or "presence" of Howells's "Editor's Study" column in *Harper's*. Urbane and highly civilized, he is like a conscientious uncle to whom time has lent perspective and an easy balance. He has known suffering and disappointment, he confides; but as an interpreter of adulthood to the young, he hastens to reassure his audience that things usually work out for the best. Those young people who consider themselves "victims of destiny" flatter themselves with a sense of their strangeness (p. 205). "The first thing you have to learn here below," he assures them, "is that in essentials you are just like every one else" (p. 205).

The same applies to Howells's boy. "I tell these things about my boy," he says, "not so much because they were peculiar to him as because I think they are, many of them, common to all boys" (p. 205). There is much in Howells's narrative to contradict this claim, however. *A Boy's Town* cannot altogether hide the fact that its author was more than once flattered (and desperately disturbed) by a sense of his own singularity. It is Howells's decorous narrator who disguises the terrors of his narrative so effectively that most readers are taken in by his assertion that the boy's near-psychotic behavior was so thoroughly normal he could have been "almost anybody's boy" (p. 2). Through this elder presence, Howells could confront the fears and alien culture of the boy with a measure of confidence because he was learning to deal with them as the anxieties of literally another person.

III

As indicated by the title, the ostensible subject of *A Boy's Town* is not so much Howells's boyhood life in Hamilton, Ohio; it is the town itself as it "appears to a boy from his third to his eleventh year" and that, between 1840 and 1849, seemed to him "peculiarly adapted for a boy to be a boy in" (pp. 1, 2). Located on western Ohio's main corridor of traffic between Cincinnati and Toledo, Hamilton could claim an unusual topography. Except for a narrow passage in the southwest corner, it was surrounded by water, and a traveler from what was then nearby Rossville could not pass through the covered bridge joining the two towns and head north without crossing water four or five times. In addition to the Great Miami River, which curved to form the town's northern and western borders, there were the Miami-Erie Canal on the east side and the canal basin jutting into the heart of the town on the south. While Howells was living in Hamilton, a hydraulic system was added to draw water from "Old River," the former channel of the Miami that left the main river at the top of its curve and formed an opposing horseshoe that dumped back into the Miami just north of the upper corporation limit. The hydraulic system provided power for Hamilton's cotton and other mills, and it included two canals of its own, besides many culverts, a large reservoir outside the town, and a small reservoir that extended into it. Naming three chapters after them, Howells traces these watercourses in such detail that the reader begins to feel as waterlogged as the boys, who "really led a kind of amphibious life . . . as long as the long summer lasted" (p. 38).

Howells is an accurate geographer; and except for the railroad, which did not replace the canal until well after Howells's family left Hamilton in 1849, *A Boy's Town* omits none of the town's major landmarks as they appear on surveyor John Crane's 1855 map of Butler County.[28] But it is in recounting the activities and prejudices of Hamilton's boys that Howells relies most heavily on what might be called his "anthropological" approach to his material, the principal technique by which he diverted attention from those troubling aspects of his boyhood that he could not face with equanimity until he was almost eighty. From the travel narratives that first established his reputation as a writer, Howells had learned not only how to describe foreign terrain but also how to capture alien folkways with the detachment of an outsider and the authority of a native. When he journeyed back into the remoteness of boyhood, therefore, it was consistent with his previous practice for Howells to adopt the viewpoint of an amateur cultural anthropologist. Accordingly, the readers of *Harper's Young People* (in which *A Boy's Town* appeared serially between April and August 1890) are introduced to this unfamiliar region through bifocal chapters with such titles as "Manners and Customs," "Plays and Pastimes," "Highdays and Holidays," "Musters and Elections," "Fantasies and Superstitions," and "Traits and Characters." Instead of the idiosyncrasies of specific boys, such chapters, including one called "The Nature of Boys," purport to teach Howells's young companions the "unwritten laws of conduct" that "come down to the boyhood of our time from the boyhood of the race" and that seem so strange to Howells in retrospect (p. 98).

Howells would gladly break this chain of inheritance and, by communicating what it was like to be a boy in his day, save young readers from repeating his mistakes. But he despairs of doing so. "Between the young and the old there is a vast gulf, seldom if ever bridged," he fears; and he must admit that in every time and place a boy's "world is all in and through the world of men and women, but no man or woman can get into it any more than if it were a world of invisible beings" (pp. 58–59, 67). In fact, Howells typically defines the culture of the boys on the basis of its absolute distinctness from adult-culture. "Everywhere and always," he says, "the world of boys is outside of the laws that govern grown-up communities" (p. 67). The boys are made aware of adult law in the form of two constables who try to prevent their swimming inside the corporation line. But

Hamilton's boys live in a constant "state of outlawry"; "savage" rather than wicked, the "natives" of the boy's town are repeatedly compared to a tribe of Indians (pp. 211–13).

It is the savagery of the boys, more than anything else, that sets their culture off from adult-culture; and Howells leaves little doubt that he sees nothing noble in this trait. Howells concedes that a boy between the ages of three and eleven may be in sight of heaven and he may see angels in the sky; but, says Howells, "he can only grope about on the earth, and he knows nothing aright that goes on there beyond his small boy's world" (p. 1). Ignorant if also innocent, the boy's relationship to that world is the unconsciously egocentric relationship of primitive man. "Like the savage," Howells writes, "he dwells on an earth round which the whole solar system revolves, and he is himself the centre of all life on the earth" (p. 6).

As for a natural appreciation of the "sublimity and beauty" of nature, that, according to Howells, is purely an acquired taste (p. 208). What a boy wants from nature is "*use*," and he is unaware of any force of inspiration within nature (p. 45). "I have often seen boys wondering at the rainbow," Howells notes, "but it was wonder, not admiration, that moved them" (p. 208). Howells thus may be taken to refute Herr Teufelsdröckh by arguing not that "the reign of wonder is done" but that it never began.[29] And he may be seen as answering his friend Sam Clemens's appeals to childhood when he adds that it is not boys who have a natural fondness for woods, fields, and rivers, but those nostalgic adults who find these things "endeared to them by association" and so think that they were once "dear for their own sakes" (p. 208).

Almost the sole positive characteristic Howells ascribes to boy-culture as opposed to adult-culture is a kind of crude social democracy. We are told that there were no questions of class or precedence in that "rude republic, where one fellow was as good as another" (p. 115). Howells recalls one curious occasion, however, when his boy descended to social savagery. For a time,

Howells's closest friend in Hamilton was a lumpish lad who "was like a piece of the genial earth" (p. 191). The two of them, Howells recalls with pre-Freudian frankness, constantly sought each other's company during the season of their friendship. They swam together for hours on end, and they lay talking endlessly on the riverbank. They could not discuss books, but young Howells "soothed" against his friend's "soft, caressing ignorance the ache of his fantastic spirit, and reposed his intensity of purpose in that lax and easy aimlessness" (p. 192). Then came the day when Howells took it upon himself to reform his playmate. Somehow he persuaded him to bathe, put on a clean shirt, and come to school. Howells publicly avowed sponsorship of the earth spirit and tried to help him get his lessons. But the experiment was doomed from the start; the friend came to school a second or third day and then did not return.

However this episode is ultimately to be interpreted, one way of regarding it is as Howells's demonstration of what happens when adult values encroach upon the non-social society of the boys. By upholding the standards of adult-culture vested in school and a clean shirt, Howells's purity as exemplar of the boys' culture is tarnished. He reveals himself to have the capacity for snobbery that will crystallize when at the age of twelve he comes to represent "society incarnate" by systematically persecuting an unmarried seamstress who sought refuge in the Howells family after being disgraced by a faithless "betrayer."[30]

Most of the time in Hamilton, however, Howells's boy represents boy-culture as it sets itself up in determined opposition to adult-culture, and one effect of Howells's anthropological technique is to give the remembered events of *A Boy's Town* the "achronic simultaneity" he once attributed to dreams.[31] Focusing on the enduring traits and timeless rituals of boy-culture, the book nearly forgets that Howells passed nine years in Hamilton. By treating his boy as an artifact, Howells complicates those elements of his narrative that contribute to making it a story of initiation and education. But the education theme is there just the same, and it embraces both the "boy in general" and the "boy in particular" that Howells said he intended "my boy" to comprehend (p. 2).

Howells's boy must attain what all boys have to attain—that "self-knowledge" which is largely the knowledge of one's limitations (p. 206). Before entering manhood, the boy must lose the egocentricity of the savage for whom the world "has no meaning but as it relates to him" (p. 6). He must give up the habit of perceiving everything as a part of his own being. To recognize no limits between himself and his environment is to fail in achieving what Howells elsewhere calls "individual existence," "a separate personality."[32]

When he defines growing up as the discovery of limitations that makes it possible to know oneself as a thing apart, Howells is celebrating almost exactly the same conception of self-knowledge Emerson bemoaned as the "Fall" of man. The place where an instinctive sense of oneness with the universe stops for the transcendentalist is also, for the realist, the place where maturity starts. And it is in the light of this definition of growing up as a growing away from unconscious egocentricity that Howells's lavish attention to the watercourses, forests, and islands of the boy's town is to be understood.

Between 1840 and 1849, the small settlement in southwestern Ohio where Howells passed his boyhood was still enclosed by a forest wall that remained "without a break except where the axe had made it" (p. 148). Although he remembers the trees to have been little cluttered by undergrowth and so more like those of a park than a forest, Howells describes them as comprising an "illimitable wilderness" (p. 25). Haunt of Solomon Whistler, who emerges almost as a Nick-of-the-woods figure, the forest is a place of mystery that takes the very soul of a boy "with love for its strangeness"; and to reach a wooded island with "especially wild" associations for Howells is to go "beyond the bounds of civilization" (pp. 149, 32). In the topography of the book, therefore, waterways delimit uncharted free territory from the region of civilized habitation. From the boys' perspective, the adult world sets up bounds and forbids trespass; and the boys' constant occupation is to break bounds, whether by going in swimming, escaping the constables, foraging in the woods, or invading an orchard. Neither members of the adult community nor wholly denizens of the wilderness, they live on the verge of both regions and both estates.

Thus the "amphibious" condition of the boys is oddly ambivalent. For while Hamilton's waterways emancipate them from the restrictions of adult culture, they cut the boys off from the safety of home and society. The waterways serve to show the protected ignorance of the boys with respect to the great world beyond the boy's town—a region, like the forest, that frightens as it allures. Howells captures the incredible insularity of childhood in a description of the covered bridge where he was once terrified of meeting Solomon Whistler:

> It is a long wooden tunnel, with two roadways, and a foot-path on either side of these; there is a toll-house at each end, and from one to the other it is about as far as from the Earth to the planet Mars. On the western shore of the river is a smaller town than the Boy's Town, and in the perspective the entrance of the bridge on that side is like a dim little doorway. (P. 24)

Although it opens upon a region as distant as those viewed nightly by astronomers, this important passageway in the boy's town shuts Howells's boy off from the vistas it discloses. It is less inviting than Thoreau's threshold to a wider world because it gives the boy an inkling of how small he is. Late in the book, after he has become an avid reader, Howells's boy will see this bridge from a changed perspective in which it appears like a bridge pictured in Howe's *History of Ohio* and so "like a bridge in some far-off country" (p. 218). But early in the narrative, he has not been exposed to the exotic reaches of literature; for the moment, his vast expanses remain closer to home. Thus the bridge, like the canal locks, requires an "awful passage" (p. 26). And although he wanders as far as the dam above the bridge, he takes years to learn that the "strange region" beyond the dam is inhabited (p. 26). Old River seems "very far away," and the island is a "measureless continent" (p. 51).[33]

As Howells's boy grows older, however, his horizons expand with his knowledge of himself and his surroundings. The child who thinks that he is the center of the town and that the town is the center of the universe learns to range beyond its limits and eventually leaves it altogether. The book opens and closes with journeys by water that constitute rites of passage from infancy to boyhood and from boyhood to adolescence. Howells's boy ages rapidly in the final chapter; and when he arrives back in Dayton after an abortive return to Hamilton, he has been transformed almost overnight into "a travelled and experienced person" (p. 246). Recognizing that the "town was small and the boys there were hemmed in by their inexperience and ignorance," Howells portrays the end of education for them as the feat of getting beyond the boundaries A Boy's Town so elaborately sets up (p. 247).

For Howells's boy as a unique personality, however, the matter is more complex. Not just the typical boy Howells says (and no doubt wanted to believe) he was, young Howells pursued in private an education that was almost directly opposed to the public education he received at the hands of the other boys. However obliquely, A Boy's Town retraces many of the crucial stages in the growth of a remarkable aesthetic consciousness. Beginning with the impression of a blossoming peach tree that he encountered in the pre-Hamilton years, Howells slowly turned inward toward a life of the imagination (p. 7). The change that came over him almost imperceptibly is described in a chapter entitled "Last Days": "That was apt to be the way with him; and before he left the Boy's Town the world within claimed him more and more. He ceased to be that eager comrade he had once been; sometimes he left his book with a sigh; and he saw much of the outer world through a veil of fancies quivering like an autumn haze between him and its realities . . . " (p. 240).

Howells had no intention of depicting his early (and increasingly exclusive) devotion to books as a budding artist's flight and fortunate escape from harsh realities inimical to art. Such a portrait would have distorted Howells's realist's image of himself. He had no intention, in other words, of writing the kind of neo-Byronic *Bildungsroman* that savored the peculiarities of a hero it took the world to task for injuring. Almost every word of Howells's formal criticism counseled against that art which dishonors external "realities" by perceiving them "through a veil of fancies." And *My Literary Passions* (1895), the literary autobiography in which Howells retold the story of his aesthetic education in greatest detail, proclaimed the most enduring works of art to be those focused squarely on the world without. Howells contrived to end his *Passions* with the name of Tolstoy because the Russian taught that art is always to be subordinated to "humanity."[34] Tolstoy embodied, in effect, the same democratic social instinct that had been the main thing Howells found to praise in the boy-culture of Hamilton.

Although it does not recommend a separation of the outside world from "the world within," however, *A Boy's Town* reveals a widening breach between the two in Howells's early life. All of the boys in Hamilton, Howells writes, *may* have been alike "in having each an inward being that was not the least like their outward being"; but he is *certain* that such was the case with his boy "and that while he was joyfully sharing the wild sports and conforming to the savage usages of the boy's world about him, he was dwelling in a wholly different world within him" (p. 171). Howells thus avowed himself to be among the "double-lived people" who allow one-half of their lives to abash them before the other (p. 184). According to Howells, his "Boy's Town life" inadvertently drove him deeper into "the Cloud Dweller's life" it refused to sanction (p. 184). (And, we may speculate, deeper into the neuroses that long survived the Hamilton experience.) By the time he left the boy's town, Howells had resolved the tension between his two lives by living largely in the world within. The trouble with this solution was that although he reigned inwardly "all thrones, principalities, and powers," he also found there the nightmare world of "grisly fancies" signified by his retention of the very early memory of a one-legged man who drowned after Howells watched him slip into the Ohio River while trying to board the steamboat carrying the Howells family to Hamilton (pp. 177, 58).

IV

Readers usually assume that water appealed to Howells's imagination as an element of healing. In *My Literary Passions*, Howells himself spoke of a therapeutic image of water travel encountered in 1858 when his psychological ills reached an early crisis. He found, he said, a lesson "of trust and courage" in the hero of Theodore Mügge's *Afraja*, who sails on and on through the fiords of Norway, always discovering a break in the surrounding high mountain walls just when escape appears hopeless. To Howells, who felt psychologically "shut in upon a mountain-walled fiord without inlet or outlet," the voyage of Mügge's young Dane occasioned "a rise in faith."[35] The arrival chapter of *Venetian Life* refers to a similar voyage in the city that must have reminded Howells of the waterways of his boy's town, however diminished by comparison: "The quick boat slid through old troubles of mine, and unlooked-for events gave it the impulse that carried it beyond, and safely around sharp corners of life."[36]

No one would deny the restorative power of these images for Howells; but they also recall the ambiguity of the boys' "amphibious" state in Hamilton. Both are images of escape; but though water carries the voyagers to safety, water is one of the perils they must evade. It was the rushing fiord as well as the high mountains that signified for Howells the circumstance of "no getting forward or going back"; the fiord cannot be omitted from that "prisoning environment" Howells hoped to be guided out of.[37] Likewise, the broad Venetian canal impressed him with "a vague feeling of anxiety." "To move on was relief; to pause was regret." Under the spell of the late hour and his reading, the new consul to Venice felt secure again only when his boat stopped and the austere door of his hotel opened upon a cheerful interior.[38]

It was still on the canal, in fact, that Howells first sensed the ambivalence, the "constant occasion for annoyance or delight, enthusiasm or sadness," that would always constitute for him the peculiar charm of Venice.[39] Quite possibly, Howells felt so much at home there because he had been schooled in contraries by a boy's life in the canals of southern Ohio; the anxious traveler on the Grand Canal seems, after all, not so far removed from the young passenger making his way to Hamilton on an Ohio River steamboat. Nor does he seem very far from independently arriving at Carl Jung's proposition that water is "the commonest symbol for the unconscious."[40] In Hamilton and Venice (or, rather, the inner pools of psychic turbulence he saw reflected in them), Howells experienced the "primitive panic" that, according to Jung, awaits the voyager who becomes lost in himself. Possibly, Howells panicked for the very reason Jung gave for our general fear of the unconscious: "because, instead of being believed in, the anxiously guarded supremacy of consciousness . . . is [in the unconscious] questioned in the most dangerous way." Indeed, Jung's description of the unconscious as "a boundless expanse full of unprecedented uncertainty" might almost have been taken from Howells's description of the ocean in *The Shadow of a Dream*.[41] After leaving Faulkner's decayed garden, Basil March had come upon "that image of eternity: the infinite waters, seasonless, changeless, boundless. The tide was still coming in, with that slow, resistless invasion of the land which is like the closing in of death upon the borders of life" (p. 35).

The psychic pressures that released a flood of reminiscence from Howells's pen between 1890 and 1900, would long outlast the recuperative exercise of writing *A Boy's Town*. Howells was trying to convince not only *Harper's* young people but himself when he wrote that "my boy used to suffer in ways that he believed no boy had ever suffered before; but as he grew older he found that boys had been suffering in exactly the same way from the beginning of time" (p. 205). To one whose vision of moral order and, beyond that, whose very sanity depended upon an exercise of self-control, that suffering may have been given a new impetus by Howells's discovery of the unconscious mind about the time his reminiscences began to be "tormented" out of him. Now when he turned within, Howells found not only the old wilderness of his neurosis; he found a new wilderness that testified that it did not matter if one was like everyone else. For even in its normal state, the deep interior of the human mind was as "savage and senseless" as Faulkner's dream or the illimitable forest outside the restrictive but reassuring lawfulness of Hamilton, Ohio. As in *The Shadow of a Dream*, a key though hidden issue in *A Boy's Town* is not whether there was substance to the disturbing day- and night-dreams of Howells's boyhood and youth; again, it is the question of control raised by the wilderness metaphor of the novel.

Howells denied any analogy between the dreamer and the writer of fiction. But he repeatedly hinted at a parallel between the dreamer and the autobiographer, whose stock in trade is "the sort of dream which all the past becomes when we try to question it."[42] Perhaps the author of *A Boy's Town* mapped the exterior world of his dream-past so meticulously because, in 1890, he still feared to question too closely that "whole region of experience—half the map of our life"—from which the dream arose. Yet if the conditions of Howells's neurosis prevented him from always confronting the painful social and sexual realities that informed the realism of Crane, Norris, and Dreiser, *A Boy's Town* showed how, by trying to learn to live with his demons, Howells prepared himself for that psychological realism to which only Henry James among his contemporaries in America contributed more profoundly.

An earlier version of this chapter appeared as "The Wilderness Within: Howells's *A Boy's Town*" in the January 1976 issue of *American Literature*. Grateful acknowledgment is made to the Duke University Press for permission to reprint it here.

1.   *Literary Friends and Acquaintance*, ed. David F. Hiatt and Edwin H. Cady (Bloomington: Indiana University Press, 1968), p. 36. Howells's "Personal Retrospect of American Authorship" first appeared in 1900.

2.   *The Quality of Mercy* (New York: Harper, 1892), p. 272.

3.   *The Rise of Silas Lapham* (Boston: Houghton Mifflin, 1885), p. 87.

4.   *My Literary Passions* and *Criticism and Fiction* (1895, 1891; rpt. 2 vols. in 1, New York: Kraus, 1968), p. 250.

5.   *A Hazard of New Fortunes*, ed. George Warren Arms (New York: Dutton, 1952), p. 540.

6.   (New York: Harper, 1888), p. 416.

7.   (New York: Harper, 1890), p. 171.

8.   "Editor's Study," *Harper's Monthly Magazine* 83 (July 1891): 315.

9.   *A Boy's Town*, p. 12.

10.   P. 417.

11.   *Harper's* 83: 315.

12.   Ibid.

13.   The story of Howells's "black time" is told in Edwin H. Cady, *The Realist at War* (New York: Syracuse University Press, 1958), pp. 56–91.

14.   *Life in Letters of William Dean Howells*, ed. Mildred Howells (New York: Doubleday, 1928), p. 129.

15.   *Years of My Youth* (New York: Harper & Bros., 1916), p. 127.

16.   *The Shadow of a Dream* and *An Imperative Duty*, ed. Martha Banta et al. (Bloomington: Indiana University Press, 1970), p. 31. All subsequent citations from the novel are to this edition and will appear in parentheses in the text.

17.   Quoted in John W. Crowley, "The Length of Howells' *Shadow of a Dream*," *Nineteenth-Century Fiction* 27 (September 1972): 192, the best essay to date on Howells's first psychological novel. The copy, probably inscribed to George Wharton Edwards, is in the collection of George Arms.

18.   On the causes of Howells's neurosis, see Edwin H. Cady, "The Neuroticism of William Dean Howells," *PMLA* 61 (1946): 229–38.

19.   *A Boy's Town*, p. 204. Subsequent references to the Harper edition of 1890 will appear in parentheses in the text.

20.   P. 59.

21.   Mitchell's response is reported in Cady, *The Road to Realism* (New York: Syracuse University Press, 1956), p. 23.

22. The earlier date is conjectured in Kenneth S. Lynn, *William Dean Howells: An American Life* (New York: Harcourt, Brace, Jovanovich, 1971), p. 333. Cady gives 1856 in *The Road to Realism*, p. 55 n.

23. *Years of My Youth*, p. 92.

24. Ibid.

25. Ibid., pp. 91, 94.

26. Cady, *The Road to Realism*, p. 70; and *Years of My Youth*, p. 167.

27. P. 94.

28. A copy of Crane's map is to be found in the Ohio Historical Society archives, Columbus, Ohio.

29. Both Thomas Carlyle and Tony Tanner were, of course, using the term *wonder* to mean what Howells signified by *admiration*.

30. *Years of My Youth*, p. 42.

31. Ibid., p. 22.

32. Ibid., pp. 3, 66.

33. Howells's poem of childhood "The Song the Oriole Sings" likewise refers to a bridge over the Miami that "Stretches its gloom from pier to pier, / Far unto alien coasts unknown."

34. *My Literary Passions*, p. 189.

35. Ibid., p. 136.

36. *Venetian Life*, 2d ed. (Boston: Osgood, 1872), p. 29.

37. *My Literary Passions*, p. 136.

38. *Venetian Life*, p. 30.

39. Ibid., p. 31.

40. *The Archetypes and the Collective Unconscious*, 2d ed., trans. R. F. C. Hull (Princeton, N.J.: Princeton University Press, 1971), p. 18.

41. Ibid., pp. 23, 21.

42. *Years of My Youth*, p. 44.

5

A Sporting Life
Henry James

> What shall we call our "self"? Where does it begin?
> Where does it end? It overflows into everything that
> belongs to us—and then flows back again.—Henry
> James, *The Portrait of a Lady* (1881)

The extent of Henry James's participation in the realistic movement has long been a matter for conjecture and inquiry. Was
James ever really a realist? Did Howells significantly influence
the art of his friend? Did James in turn affect the course of
American realism in any way? The critics, as a rule, have raised
such questions only to affirm James's part in the dominant literary movement of his generation. Howells's portrait of "Henry
James, Jr.," in the *Century Magazine* for November 1882 declared James to be the "chief exemplar" in English of a new
school of fiction "largely influenced" by the realism of Daudet;[1]
and a year later in the same magazine James himself characterized French fiction as dwelling on "the actual," "the sensible,"
"the concrete." The "main object of the novel," he explained,
"is to represent life."[2] Seen in this context, James's great essay
of 1884, "The Art of Fiction," appears to be a realistic docu-
ment and (along with his essay on Turgenev of the same year)
justifies Leon Edel's more recent assertion that James "was
to consider himself, and to be considered, one of the new realists of American fiction."[3]

The two volumes of Edel's *Henry James* that cover the period of realism's dominance in American literature suggest little cause for revising the traditional view that James and Howells, without altogether intending it, stood together as brother realists in the mid-1880s. But other volumes of the Edel biography, particularly *The Treacherous Years*, provide considerable evidence of a convergence in the thought of the two men *later* in their respective careers than is usually supposed. Instead of drifting apart in all but personal regard soon after the high tide of the realistic movement, they were drawn closer in their art in the fullness of a time fraught with challenges and trials for both.

James first met Howells in Cambridge in 1866 when Howells came East to join the staff of the *Atlantic Monthly*; and the two young men (Howells was twenty-nine years old, James twenty-three) occasionally took long, "literary" walks together until James's passionate pilgrimage to Europe intervened in 1869 (the year, incidentally, of Howells's first meeting with Mark Twain). Yet it is clear that James had reservations about Howells as a writer almost from the beginning of their acquaintance. Speaking to Grace Norton about Howells's "slender primitive capital," James wrongly predicted that Howells was "destined to fade slowly and softly away in self-repetition and reconcilement to the commonplace."[4] To Charles Eliot Norton, around the same time, he confided the belief that Howells lacked the "really *grasping* imagination" necessary for wresting art from the meager American scene. "To write well and worthily of American things one need even more than elsewhere to be a *master*. But unfortunately, one is less!"[5] The "one," James made apparent, referred to Howells.

Also in the early seventies, James alluded to a "pathetic discordance" in his friend's talent—"the need of applying really first-class handling to subjects belonging to *la petite littérature*." Writers like Howells, he charged, transferred the "crude accidents" of life directly into their fiction without sufficient "intellectual transmutation."[6] Here James rested for a moment upon the ground that would separate him permanently from the realistic movement and temporarily from its chief advocate in America. James's quarrel with Howells's art was not just that its province could be too limited. His 1886 essay in *Harper's Weekly* chided Howells because he appeared "to hold composition too cheap." Adoring "the common, the immediate, the familiar," Howells sacrificed "the effect that comes from alternation, distribution, relief."[7] This was James's criticism as well of the Russian novelists whom Howells so much admired. Tolstoy and Dostoyevsky wrote "loose baggy monsters" and "fluid puddings" precisely because they ignored the fine arts of selection and distribution. So even when Howells approached the scope of the Russians in *A Hazard of New Fortunes*, James praised the book's abundance—"so beyond what he at one time seemed in danger of reducing himself to"—yet he accused Howells of turning his back on "the matter of composition."[8] Howells achieved an expanded perspective, James felt, by throwing overboard many questions of form and style; for his part, James was "perpetually trying to fish them up."[9]

The two writers, however, were then perhaps more fundamentally in accord than ever before—including that *annus mirabilis* of realism, 1885-86. It was William James who recognized the importance of 1890 for American literary history; that August he wrote to Howells: "The year which shall have witnessed the apparition of your *Hazard of New Fortunes*, of Harry's *Tragic Muse*, and of my *Psychology* will indeed be a memorable one in American Literature!!"[10] The psychologist-philosopher could have been more farsighted only had he observed that 1890 was also the year of *The Shadow of a Dream* and *A Boy's Town*. For at almost the same moment Howells was emerging from his "black time" to write autobiographical narratives of a disturbed past, James was entering upon the "treacherous years" that eventually sent him back to childhood before he too emerged to achieve a new psychic strength and a new kind of fiction.

The equivalent for James of Howells's black time and its aftermath was the entire decade of the nineties, but especially the years from 1890 to 1895, during which James concentrated on the drama.[11] James had neither the wife nor daughter whose misfortunes helped plunge Howells into another lasting depression; but by the time he too reached early middle age, it came home to James that he alone must bear the responsibility of providing for his invalid sister, Alice. In 1892, Alice James died, easing her brother's family burden but dissolving one of the privileged relationships of James's life. Less than two years later, James's confidante, Fenimore Woolson, committed suicide—in part, Edel implies, because James rejected her. And one year after that, James's ill-fated play, *Guy Domville*, earned the scarcely suppressed ridicule of a large portion of the audience on opening night. James left the theater in a mood like those that had descended upon Howells in his "black time." The weeks immediately following *Guy Domville*, James wrote Howells in March 1896, "were weeks of black darkness for me."[12] James had come to doubt his creative powers; his reputation as a novelist had been eroded by five years of too exclusive devotion to the theater; and he was feeling deserted both by personal friends and by the reading public. "You put your finger sympathetically on the place and spoke of what I wanted you to speak of," he told Howells. "I *have* felt, for a long time past, that I have fallen upon evil days—every sign or symbol of one's being in the least *wanted*, anywhere or by any one, having so utterly failed."[13]

James responded to this crisis of confidence much as Howells had responded to the climax of his own evil days: he turned to autobiographical forms in an effort to combat the psychological furies that threatened him and his identity as a writer. James's therapeutic writings were not avowedly personal at first. They were disguised as fiction, particularly the fictional histories of little girls; but they were no less autobiographical and no less concerned with childhood than Howells's boy-book of 1890. Before *Guy Domville* failed, James had shown no unusual proclivity for the very young. Beginning, however, with *The Other House* (1896), and continuing with *What Maisie Knew* (1897), *The Turn of the Screw* (1898), *The Awkward Age* (1899), and a number of short stories, James gave his imagination over to the fears and elations of children and adolescents. What is more, James produced his tales of childhood in the remarkable sequence Edel discerns when he writes that James's "precocious little females grow a little older in each story, as if they were a single child whose life experience is being traced from the cradle to coming-of-age."[14] In this restorative sequence, according to Edel, one can make out "an extensive personal allegory of the growing up of Henry James" (who remembered the protective feminine disguises he had adopted as a precocious little boy). By "reliving the long-ago 'education' of his emotions," James like Freud "could move forward into new depths of adult experience."[15]

The success of James's subliminal self-healing through the writing of autobiographical fiction may be measured by the composure of the avowedly autobiographical works on which this chapter centers. *A Small Boy and Others* (1913), *Notes of a Son and Brother* (1914), and *The Middle Years* (1917) were set down near the end of James's life, long after he had sufficiently regained his self-esteem to produce the great novels of the major phase. Yet even these late autobiographical volumes, with their quality of acceptance and of triumphs secured, convey a sense of self-discovery along with their confident recapitulation. James still appears to be reassuring himself that he had been right to stand apart from the "others" in his life and that "there had been in a manner continuity, been not so much waste as one had sometimes ruefully figured."[16]

I

Perhaps the most striking feature of the two volumes and fragment of a third that make up James's autobiography is their author's astonishingly fertile (and largely accurate) play of memory. When he began dictating in the winter of 1911, James had no fund of documents from his childhood and early youth to draw on. "No preliminary work was needed," wrote his amanuensis Theodora Bosanquet. "A straight dive into the past brought to the surface treasure after treasure."[17] As James continued to be overtaken by the ghosts of the past, he came more and more to rely on documentation. *A Small Boy and Others*, according to Miss Bosanquet, "was finished before bringing William to an age for writing letters"; but William was seventeen at the start of the period covered by *Notes of a Son and Brother*, and Henry was beguiled by the appeal of letters from his brothers and father to reproduce them, somewhat edited, at considerable length in the text. Thus it is difficult not to agree with James's suspicion that to open the door into "the limbo of old letters, charged with their exquisite ghostly appeal, is almost to sink into depths of concession."[18]

However, like Ralph Pendrel in *The Sense of the Past*, James too "wanted evidence of a sort for which there had never been documents enough."[19] Even *Notes of a Son and Brother*, as Frederick W. Dupee has said, returns after painting its fine partial portraits to James's most compelling subject—his own consciousness.[20] And *A Small Boy and Others* can stand beside the best American examples of the education form because James was well aware of the danger of losing himself and his reader in either a mass of letters or the golden haze of memory. Reminiscence required order and control if it was to be something more than mere retreat into the "vieux temps": "If one tries to evoke," James insisted, "one must neglect none of the arts, one must do it with all the forms" (p. 38). Consequently, James endeavored wherever possible in the autobiography to string the "apparently dispersed and disordered parts" of his narrative upon "a fine silver thread" (p. 454).

One coarser thread binding James's narrative together is chronology. Except for passing references to the family's stay in Europe soon after his birth in April 1843, volume 1 chronicles the decade, 1845–55, of James's early-Victorian childhood in Albany and New York City. Much of this time James spent in those American "dispensaries of learning" that his parents forsook in June 1855 for the highly esteemed Swiss schools of the day. James is fourteen years old when *A Small Boy and Others* ends with the attack of typhus that struck him in Boulogne-sur-Mer in 1857. Volume 2, opening with the family's re-establishment at Geneva in 1859, continues the account of contacts with European schools; but in chapter 4, the scene shifts to Newport, that "remedial" halfway house for Europeanized Americans to which the expatriates returned a second time late in 1860. Most of the volume recounts the war years and is devoted to the portraits of brothers, father, and family friends that James drew with the aid of letters in his possession. (For the sake of "tone," James sometimes departs from strict chronology, grouping letters from a broad time span in clusters about central figures. The three chapters devoted to his father at the center of the volume, for instance, contain examples of the elder James's correspondence dating from the early 1840s to the late 1870s.) The volume ends with the death of James's favorite cousin, Minny Temple, in 1870. Her passing was a fitting conclusion, James says; the brothers "felt it together as the end of our youth" (p. 544).

Overlapping slightly in time with *Notes of a Son and Brother*, *The Middle Years* opens in 1869 with James's first independent trip to Europe. Although this fragment recalls incidents that occurred almost ten years later, James lived to complete only six short chapters and a portion of a seventh. Despite this permanent break in chronology, however, the autobiography seems essentially complete. The historical sequence of events was of only secondary concern, and a final lapse in chronology did not prevent James from giving ample play to a more important principle of selection. That silver thread, James said, "the principle governing, by my measure, these recoveries and reflections," was "the recording and figuring act on behalf of some case of the imaginative faculty under cultivation" (p. 454).

Such a subject had always interested the author of *The Ambassadors*, and he was to stumble belatedly upon the ideal case: "He had been with me all the while, and only too obscurely and intimately," James observes in the autobiography. "I had in a word to draw him forth from within rather than meet him in the world before me, the more convenient sphere of the objective, and to make him objective, in short, had to turn nothing less than myself inside out. What was *I* thus, within and essentially, what had I ever been and could I ever be but a man of imagination at the active pitch?" (p. 455). When he was bringing *Notes of a Son and Brother* to a close, James could look back over the bulk of what was to become the published autobiography; and from that vantage he recognized that he had written the "personal history, as it were, of an imagination" (p. 454).

II

Since it studies the imaginative life "under cultivation," the general movement of the autobiography is from isolated images to complex clusters of images as James deals with a more and more recent past and as his small boy develops the unifying instinct of the artist. Volume 1 opens with fragmentary glimpses of the disfurnished American stage—William bent forward over a table, the "bright blur" of a school run by a Miss Bayou or Bayhoo, the white stone steps and fan-lighted door of the Albany house at No. 50 North Pearl Street, the New York state capitol building beneath spreading trees. Gradually the book develops nuclei around which such fragments cluster—that portion of old New York bounded by Union Square and Washington Square and by Fifth and Sixth Avenues; the houses first at No. 21 Washington Place and later at No. 58 West Fourteenth Street near Sixth Avenue; miscellaneous schoolrooms and teachers; a stretch of Fifth Avenue near the southwest corner of Ninth Street

where theater playbills were posted. (This latter is particularly
central in a narrative that devotes perhaps an eighth of its pages
to reminiscences of the theater.)

At any time, James's narrator is capable of intruding to give
such fragments compositional harmony, as he does by making
"a drama of the delicate" out of his great-aunt Helen Wyckoff's
manipulations of her brother Henry and her "spectral spouse"
(p. 85). In the narrator's hands, these relationships, the germ
of James's play *The Reprobate*, are worked toward a self-con-
scious denouement; the musings of the small boy as distinct
from those of James's narrator, however, are not so elaborately
structured at first. His earliest memory, for example, is reported
in a single sentence which maintains that James kept a distinct
impression from the family's visit to Paris before he was two
years old. Recalling a carriage ride in which he sat in long
baby clothes on the seat opposite his parents, James further recalls being "impressed with the view, framed by the clear window of the vehicle as we passed, of a great stately square surrounded with high-roofed houses and having in its centre a tall
and glorious column" (p. 32). The square was the Place Ven-
dôme; and the column, the grand *colonne* raised in honor of
Napoleon's victories. These monuments to the empire stood as
fitting emblems of the shining city that dazzled Hyacinth
Robinson in *The Princess Casamassima* and that both attracted
and appalled the future novelist who at age twelve would again
confront the glorious insolence of Paris in visits to the Louvre.
But square and column are barely sketched here. Consisting of
but two primary elements, the view is relatively spare even
though as an early memory of aesthetic illumination it invites all
sorts of contrasts with Howells's peach blossoms. It is James
the narrator rather than the remarkably small boy who gives
this scene the faintest outlines of a picture "framed" by the
carriage window.

One of the most scenic memories in volume 1 of the autobiography is recorded a chapter later as James calls up father

and son strolling together along the New York dockside. The small boy takes in the summer heat, the loose cobbles of the pavement, and the black mud. Then his eager appetite, almost a presence in the book, is aroused by succulent provisions stacked on wharves and streets. The passage ends with an encomium on peaches: "Above all the public heaps of them, the high-piled receptacles at every turn, touched the street as with a sort of southern plenty; the note of the rejected and scattered fragments, the memory of the slippery skins and rinds and kernels with which the old dislocated flags were bestrown, is itself endeared to me and contributes a further pictorial grace" (p. 42). For the moment this is as close as the small boy comes to producing a composition. Even the "epoch-making" occasion seven chapters later when he hears a brash little cousin warned against making a "scene" is recalled in relatively scanty detail, although the incident carried with it the "immense illumination" that one could make scenes or not as one chose (p. 107).

The actors and settings of James's personal drama do not remain permanently dim and undeveloped, however. In chapter 20 of *A Small Boy and Others*, James's remembered impressions become more complicated when he recalls the family's European sojourn of 1855–58. Again on a carriage ride, James encounters a view that struck him all his life "as crucial, as supremely determinant" (p. 159). The carriage has paused at a village somewhere on the road between Lyons and Geneva, and twelve-year-old Henry, suffering from a fever, raises himself from his traveling couch to witness a tableau that presents more "character" than he has hitherto felt in any scene. At the end of the village street, he sees a ruined castle, and laboring on the intervening slope, a peasant woman in sabots—the first peasant he has ever beheld. Here in a single "ecstatic vision" is Europe "expressed and guaranteed" to him. Castle, ruin, and peasant flow into a "sublime synthesis," and the sick boy wonders at "the whole consistency" of the enchanted scene. "It made," James says, "a bridge over to more things than I then knew" (p. 161).

One other "bridge" of critical importance in the autobiography is the Louvre, "educative, formative, fertilising," James considered it, to a degree no other place could rival (p. 197). In this hushed yet crowded temple, life and art became "mixed and interchangeable"; here the young pilgrim looked at pictures, but he also "looked at France and looked at Europe, looked even at America as Europe itself might be conceived so to look, looked at history, as a still-felt past and a complacently personal future, at society, manners, type, characters, possibilities and prodigies and mysteries of fifty sorts" (pp. 198, 199). Consisting of many more than two lone aspects, or even than three aspects richly remembered and elaborately composed, the Louvre provided "a splendid scene" where almost anything could happen (p. 196).

The most intriguing mystery surrounding James's small boy arises in the Louvre's Galerie d'Apollon, rebuilt for Louis XIV after it burned in 1661 and housing Delacroix frescoes, crown jewels, Byzantine mosaics, and such heroic canvases as Géricault's *Raft of the "Medusa"*. With its high coved ceiling and polished floor, the 200-foot long gallery seemed to form a huge tube or tunnel through which young James inhaled "a general sense of *glory*" (p. 196). For a consciousness just aborning to the splendors of European culture, the Galerie d'Apollon constituted a "bridge over to Style" (p. 196). But it would be a long time before the gallery offered up its most personal and startling associations for James. He had first visited the Louvre in July 1855, some weeks before the family passed through the nameless village of the castle, ruin, and peasant. Yet James's narrative takes up this shrine out of chronological order near the end of *A Small Boy and Others* because it was to be the scene "in a summer dawn many years later" of an extraordinary nightmare (p. 196).

As reported in the autobiography, the climax of James's nightmare was "the sudden pursuit, through an open door, along a huge high saloon, of a just dimly-descried figure that retreated in terror before my rush and dash" (p. 196). Rapidly becoming a "diminished spot in the long perspective," the figure escapes, and James gloats over his triumph of aggression (p. 197). He has turned the tables on the visitant by barring him from a chamber that he himself had "a moment before been desperately, and all the more abjectly, defending by the push of my shoulder against hard pressure on lock and bar from the other side" (pp. 196–97). The strength of his defensive impulse is something to wonder at, but the "point" of the whole dream, James says, is exactly *where* it is shown to transpire. As he watches the figure disappear through the glare of lightning outside a row of high windows, the "lightning that revealed the retreat revealed also the wondrous place and, by the same amazing play, my young imaginative life in it of long before, the sense of which, deep within me, had kept it whole, preserved it to this thrilling use; for what in the world were the deep embrasures and the so polished floor but those of the Galerie d'Apollon of my childhood? The 'scene of something' I had vaguely then felt it? Well I might, since it was to be the scene of that immense hallucination" (p. 197).

No two readers will agree altogether on what James's immense hallucination means. Clearly it indicates that impulses deep within him had irrepressibly asserted James's right to a central place not only in the temple of art and culture but of "history and fame and power, the world in fine raised to the richest and noblest expression" (p. 196). The glory of the Louvre encompassed all these things, and at first it had simply overwhelmed the little American pilgrim. Slowly, however, under pressure of frequently renewed contact, the Louvre had been made to give up its treasures. The "small sacred consciousness" had learned to assimilate the many presences that swarmed there for it (p. 198). Instead of merely guarding the door to the temple, that consciousness had expelled forces threatening to expel it and had aggressively taken possession of the interior. James's small boy was to become anything but a "poor" Hyacinth Robinson, excluded from the circles of light that could nourish a fastidious imagination.

Leon Edel, in a refinement of this basic interpretation of the dream, has gone so far as to suggest an identity for James's visitant. Noting that James's account of the nightmare immediately follows an account of extended walks in the company of his older brother, Edel speculates that the apparition was inspired by William James.[21] Throughout the autobiography, Henry is forever citing young William's superior talent and achievement. In the first chapter, for example, he writes, "I never for all the time of childhood and youth in the least caught up with him or overtook him. He was always round the corner and out of sight . . . " (pp. 7–8). No doubt sibling rivalry took its toll on James's youthful psyche; and though the autobiography suppresses any hint of a sustained jealousy in the small boy, there must have been times when William's easy superiority even in painting and drawing, not to mention "scientific" studies, seemed particularly galling. If the figure in the nightmare was William James—which might explain why Henry's dread of him was "irresistible" but "shameful"—the significant thing about William's being round the corner and out of sight was that, this time, Henry put him there (p. 196). (Frequent testimonials to William's genius notwithstanding, Henry managed to rout his older brother in another way in the autobiography. The book that started as an "attempt to place together some particulars of the early life of William James" rapidly became Henry's story and only secondarily the story of the others in his orbit [p. 3].)

III

The faintly eerie account of a nightmare inspired by his conquest of the Louvre belonged, of course, to the consciousness of the aging writer who set it down when he was past seventy. It was no more the work of a twelve-year-old boy than the nightmare itself, which sprang from the subconscious of a man "many years" his senior. But one could easily read the closing chapters of *A Small Boy and Others* without becoming fully aware that James's "scene of something" combined impressions from three widely different periods of his life. Probably, James let his impressions merge because he was paying homage to the young imaginative life whose memory he kept intact through all those years. The hours in the Louvre, James made clear, had been part "of the vague processes . . . of picking up an education," and the autobiography strained to the point of falsifying the record in its zeal to prove the consistency of that training (p. 199).[22]

Moreover, James imbued his nightmare with the dense texture of one of his late short stories (complete with Jamesian title) because he had brought the young imagination of his narrative to the threshold of scenic composition. Soon after reconstructing the wonderful nightmare and before signifying a total if temporary lapse of consciousness in the fever that marked the end of his boyhood, James's narrative has developed in the small boy the "lively felt need that everything should represent something more than what immediately and all too blankly met the eye. . . . What I wanted, in my presumption, was that the object, the place, the person, the unreduced impression . . . should give out to me something of a situation" (pp. 231–32). At age fourteen, the boy has begun to look about him with the eye of the novelist; and when *Notes of a Son and Brother* opens in his sixteenth year, he can grasp a scene, "round it and make it compose" because he has made a crucial discovery:

> To feel a unity, a character and a tone in one's impressions, to feel them related and all harmoniously coloured, that *was* positively to face the aesthetic, the creative, even, quite wondrously, the critical life and almost on the spot to commence author. They had begun, the impressions—that was what was the matter with them—to scratch quite audibly at the door of liberation, of extension, of projection. . . . (P. 253)

That impressions flowed easily for him, James says he more or less knew even at age sixteen. Why they flowed, however, was a question he would have to wait some time to answer. James's boy does not begin practicing the profession antici- pated here until ten chapters later, near the conclusion of the second volume of the autobiography. But he is already con- firmed in that profession because he is the product of a unique education.

Under the influence of his father's arduous optimism and distaste for business, James grew up being told that the usual careers and professions were "narrowing." Commenting on the "precious metal" he and his brothers were to strive for, he re- membered not the faintest hint that they were to seek "the refined gold of 'success' " (p. 123). To the elder James, all edu- cational method was suspect except his own, which boiled down to a single alchemic word: "Convert, convert, convert!" "We were to convert and convert," James remembered, "success . . . or no success; and simply everything that should happen to us, every contact, every impression and every experience we should know, were to form our soluble stuff . . . " (p. 123).

The educational "method" of James's "spiritually perceiving and responding sire" becomes intelligible when placed against the background of the Swedenborgian philosophy on which he lectured and wrote after the works of the Swedish mystic re- stored him to spiritual health following a severe "vastation" in 1844 (p. 395). The method of Swedenborg was like that of the transcendentalism that learned from him; for even rigid Swedenborgianism, while insisting on one-to-one relationships between divine realities and appearances in the material world, did its work by appeal to the doctrine of correspondence. The Swedenborgian's task was to perceive correspondences be- tween natural facts and spiritual facts, thereby *converting* both into spiritual truth. The Swedenborgian who once told Emerson he was led "to seek the *laws* of these appearances that swim round us in God's great museum" freely accepted Emerson's dictum that, under proper cultivation, "it is the constant ten- dency of the mind to unify all it beholds" (p. 345).[23]

Henry James, Jr., and his brothers did not dip into their father's ideas in written form until William James performed the filial piety of editing *The Literary Remains of the Late Henry James* (1884). They did not need to, James tells us, because they drank deeply "at the source itself" (p. 331). And though all who lived near James's father were "thrown so upon the inward life" that they could not avoid the lesson of conversion, none of the elder James's children had a greater innate capacity for conversion or a greater susceptibility to the inward life than his second son (p. 35). Henry James, Jr., grew up believing that there were simply two different ways of taking life. One way "was to go in for everything and everyone," and "the other way was to be as occupied, quite as occupied, just with the sense and the image of it all" (p. 164). If brothers William and Wilkie were immersers in their different fashions, Henry was to take the second approach to life. Thus at the outset of the autobiography, he pictures himself "wondering and dawdling and gaping," a small boy for whom contemplation took the place of action (p. 17). "He is a convenient little image or warning of all that was to be for him, and he might well have been even happier than he was. For there was the very pattern and measure of all he was to demand: just to *be* somewhere—almost anywhere would do—and somehow receive an impression or an accession, feel a relation or a vibration" (p. 17). Feel it, that is, and transform it in the chamber of his sensibility. For, like Emerson and Thoreau, James strove to convert the sense data of consciousness into revelation. And like Emerson's poet, he was the seer and purveyor of vision who writes late in the second volume of the autobiography that "when one should cease to live in large measure by one's eyes (with the imagination of course all the while waiting on this) one would have taken the longest step towards not living at all" (p. 443). For the staring boy as for Emerson, sight was the primary sense; and even the quality of his vision resembled Emerson's.

When James's boy begins to feel "a unity, a character and a

tone" in his impressions and finds them "related and all har-
moniously coloured," he is on the verge of becoming Emerson's
"Man Thinking" and of validating his father's educational
theory. If it does nothing else, the education of James's boy
shows him to have been possessed of the "root of the matter"
as his father defined it, that is, "the matter of our having with
considerable intensity *proved* educable, or, if you like better,
teachable, that is accessible to experience" (p. 124). What
James meant by his key terms can best be explained by the
definitions of such concepts as "impressions" and "experience"
he imbedded in "The Art of Fiction." Here is the famous
spider-web image from that essay:

> Experience is never limited, and it is never complete; it is an immense
> sensibility, a kind of huge spider-web of the finest silken threads
> suspended in the chamber of consciousness, and catching every
> air-borne particle in its tissue. It is the very atmosphere of the
> mind; and when the mind is imaginative—much more when it hap-
> pens to be that of a man of genius—it takes to itself the faintest hints
> of life, it converts the very pulses of the air into revelations. . . .
> If experience consists of impressions, it may be said that impres-
> sions *are* experience, just as (have we not seen it?) they are the very
> air we breathe.[24]

In this image of himself as a receptacle (or, more accurately,
a reflector) of impressions and in his insistence that true education consists of accessibility to experience, itself a network of
impressions, James reveals how close he was to adopting the
essentials of a transcendental epistemology.

It must be added, however, that Emerson's philosophical
idealism was no more available to James finally than to Adams,
Clemens, or Howells. James did not come to share Adams's
late sense of chaos and dissolution, but neither did he partici-
pate in the "noble" doubts of Emerson's hypothetical transcendentalist about the outward existence of the universe.
James was sincere in telling his brother that "pragmatism"
represented his philosophy too. The metaphor of the house of

fiction like the metaphor of the spider web testified that life "out there" was a "given" for James. Significant meaning resided no more exclusively in the apocalypse of the mind than in "the thing of accident, of mere actuality, still unappropriated" (p. 150). James's spider web originated no flies. Even if there were no other evidence in James's autobiography, the images drawn from the plastic and dramatic arts would reveal a key difference between James's aesthetic idealism and the idealism of his predecessors. The process that had shaped Emerson's Man Thinking had been education by nature; contemplating the unity of nature, he had been led to the higher truth that nature, man, and divinity are one. When in the autobiography James does occasionally recall communing with nature, his treatment of the New England landscape could not contrast more sharply with Emerson's or Thoreau's.

James's reminiscences on one such rare occasion are associated with John LaFarge's landscape studies of Newport. (It was LaFarge who advised James to give up painting in favor of writing and who later urged Henry Adams to give up writing for painting.) James remembers accompanying LaFarge to an "umbrageous valley" where "a spell of romance rested for several hours on our invocation of the genius of the scene" (p. 297). In the "rustling murmuring green and plashing water and woodland voices and images" of the glen, James was reminded of "a passage of old poetry, a scrap of old legend" (p. 297). The "radiance" and "sweetness of solitude" of rocky coastal promontories and pastures "amounted in themselves to the highest 'finish' " (p. 300). And the entire area was a "kind of boundless empty carpeted saloon" (p. 300). Far from concluding with the young Emerson that nature is "the representative of the universal mind" and that "Art must be a complement to nature, strictly subsidiary,"[25] James says that the Newport landscape, "locally regarded as our scenery," was to be cherished for "its scale and constitution" and for "the adorable wise economy with which nature had handled it" (p. 299). For

James, then, the natural scene was "scenery," and what one hoped to learn from it was compositional harmony. As F. O. Matthiessen has said, James "turned that double-edged word 'seer' back to this world."[26]

He turned it in particular to those aspects of the world displaying pictorial value. When in the autobiography James at last embraced his calling and the medium suiting his personal talent, "it was to feel, with reassurance, that the picture was still after all in essence one's aim" (p. 150). This consistency explains why the autobiography, like James's fiction, is so full of scenes; and it also explains why James made no hard distinction between scenes drawn from the dramatic, as distinct from the plastic or verbal, arts. All the arts were unified in their power to body forth what the artist's sensibility joined together —"that pictorial which was ever . . . the dramatic, the social, the effectively human aspect" (p. 482). Indeed, the autobiography makes little distinction between representative life and presented art, or between art as a mode of expression and art as a mode of seeing. In one remarkable passage, in fact, James actually fuses the organ of sight with the place where scenes are usually played out. Noting that his earliest attempts at writing had been on folded quarto sheets with three pages of text and a fourth of drawing—that is, in "dramatic, accompanied by pictorial composition"—James recalls how his juvenile scenes "flowered at every pretext into the very optic and perspective of the stage, where the boards diverged correctly [in his drawings], from a central point of vision, even as the lashes from an eyelid, straight down to the footlights" (pp. 148, 49). James had turned the word "seer" back to the world of art.

IV

Repeatedly in the autobiography, James pictures himself groping through a dim forest. "I have to disengage my mantle here with a force in which I invite my reader to believe," he says at one point, "for I push through a thicket of memories

in which the thousand-fingered branches arrestingly catch"
(p. 497). At another time, he brushes aside a "branch" of the
matter engaging him (p. 122). And on still another occasion,
he describes his record as "a tale of assimilations small and
fine" out of which "the most branching vegetations may be
conceived as having sprung" (p. 105). Such metaphors, suggesting the interconnectedness of vision, the roots running
under ground, that Emerson cultivated, establish one of James's
chief ties to a transcendental heritage. Another is suggested by
a group of related metaphors. About midway through *Notes of
a Son and Brother*, James remembers himself in youth as "a
novelist *en herbe*" (p. 373). Further, he several times reminds
readers that he is tracing the growth of his subject's "aesthetic
seeds"; and in a different context, he declares the beauty of
anything worth illustrating (including, presumably, the history
of an imagination) to lie in its "developments; and developments, alas, are the whole flowering of the plant" (pp. 95,
480).

If we take such metaphors of growth as metaphors for the
expanding consciousness, they appear to link James more directly to those Americans of the mid-nineteenth century who
wrote "organic" narratives of "cultivation" than to those
members of his own generation who turned to the education
form. Almost from the moment the gaping boy opens his eyes
or his folded quarto sheets, he foreshadows the master novelist
still relying on his vision and the imagination behind it. Boy
and man converge because James's life, as he recollected it,
enjoyed a continuity lacking in the autobiographies of Adams,
Clemens, or even Howells. It would be a mistake, however, to
conclude that James was left untouched by the changing views
of human psychology that influenced the autobiographies of
his contemporaries. For one thing, James's book demonstrated
that the skill of composing in scenes was developed only
through time, not beyond or above it. Furthermore, his forest
metaphor testified to James's interest in a field of inquiry that
Emerson never penetrated.

James's subject in the autobiography is not so much his past as the play of his present imagination in the act of recapturing its past history. As a result, perhaps no other American autobiography reconstitutes so palpably the very atmosphere of the mind that "The Art of Fiction" declared to be the seat of experience. And in this atmosphere, James's wonderful nightmare of the Louvre is suffused with yet another glow of suggestion. What the Louvre offered James foremost when he first visited it in 1855 was "a heart-shaking little prevision" of the future (p. 197). It intimated the kind of life that one who dedicated himself to the pursuit of culture was going to lead. Though the small boy did not then have the term, it promised a life "tremendously 'sporting' in its way" (p. 198). The heroic forms of the gallery, the "continuity of honour" between initial visit and long-delayed nightmare, a general tendency on James's part to glorify such passages by casting them in the language of adventure, and especially the decisive burst of inner force behind his utter overthrow of the appalling challenger, all these things suggest James's habit of equating acts of "cogitation and comparison" with outbursts of "life-saving energy" (p. 196). James's "dream-adventure" (he used the term his friend Robert Louis Stevenson had applied long before in a discussion of dreams) took place only in the mind.[27] But James held the most sporting of all lives to be that of the circling, stalking, exploring consciousness. If the beasts that sprang on his introspective fictional characters sprang from the jungles within, they forced crises nonetheless real, and so nonetheless demanding of "life-saving energy," for their being in a double sense imaginary. James's account of his nightmare was but another of his fables proposing that a man of imagination at the highest pitch should also be taken for a man of action at the highest pitch. It demonstrated that the life of the visiting mind ("the only form of riot or revel ever known to me," James said) could be made to pass for, and could actually be, a life of high adventure (p. 16).

In this light, even the relatively sedentary enterprise of stalk-

ing one's personal past—a pursuit James actively followed from
the publication of *The American Scene* in 1907 through the
third volume of the autobiography—threatened to become a
most dangerous game. "Recovering the lost was at all events
on this scale," says Ralph Pendrel of the fragmentary *Sense of
the Past*, "much like entering the enemy's lines to get back
one's dead for burial."[28] The "mild apparitionism" of reminiscence and the dense forest of memory held pitfalls to be evaded
only by the steadiest courage and the coolest strategy, for the
past that would trap the hero of James's unfinished novel
threatened also to make a prisoner of the autobiographer who
penetrated too deep and too long (p. 54). Like Howells, James
was straying into the wilderness of the unconscious.

It was perhaps a reflexive urge to protect his own psychic
integrity that led James to misremember the short story he had
based on his dream of the Louvre. In his notebook in 1914,
James wrote of "The Jolly Corner": "My hero's adventure
there takes the form so to speak of his turning the tables, as
I think I called it, on a 'ghost' or whatever, a visiting or haunt-
ing apparition otherwise qualified to appall *him*; and thereby
winning a sort of victory by the appearance, and the evidence,
that this personage or presence was more overwhelmingly affected by him than he by *it*."[29]   What James had remembered
in 1914 was not, of course, the short story in which Spencer
Brydon is almost destroyed by his visitant; it was the nightmare
as interpreted in the autobiographical volume of the year before. "The lucidity, not to say the sublimity, of the crisis,"
James wrote in *A Small Boy and Others*, "had consisted of the
great thought that I, in my appalled state, was probably still
more appalling than the awful agent, creature or presence,
whatever he was, whom I had guessed, in the suddenest wild
start from sleep, the sleep within my sleep, to be making for
my place of rest" (p. 197). This was wish fulfillment, or at least
wishful thinking. Like "The Jolly Corner," James's autobiography was a residuum of the psychic distress of the treacherous

years, and even there James could not venture into the depths of his unconscious without fleeting doubts about returning psychically intact. Whether he imagined the world within as a house of rooms, a forest, or a jungle, he was still establishing sovereignty over that realm of experience which his friend Howells also entered in old age only as hard-won territory.

1. Edwin H. Cady, ed., *W. D. Howells as Critic* (London and Boston: Routledge & Kegan Paul, 1973), pp. 70, 71.

2. *Century Magazine* 26 (August 1883): 501, 506.

3. *Henry James: The Conquest of London* (Philadelphia and New York: Lippincott, 1962), p. 168 (hereafter cited as *The Conquest of London*).

4. Quoted in Leon Edel, *Henry James: The Untried Years* (Philadelphia and New York: Lippincott, 1953), p. 273 (hereafter cited as *The Untried Years*). The date of James's letter was November 1870.

5. Percy Lubbock, ed., *The Letters of Henry James* (New York: Scribner's, 1920), 1:30-31.

6. Quoted in Edel, *The Conquest of London*, p. 23.

7. *Harper's Weekly* 30 (19 June 1886): 394, 395.

8. Edel, *The Untried Years*, p. 272; Lubbock, *Letters*, 1:165.

9. Edel, *The Untried Years*, p. 272.

10. Quoted in F. O. Matthiessen, *The James Family* (New York: Knopf, 1947), p. 508.

11. Edel refers principally to the second half of this decade in *Henry James: The Treacherous Years* (Philadelphia and New York: Lippincott, 1969) (hereafter cited as *The Treacherous Years*); as Edel describes them, however, these were years of therapy and healing. It was during the period 1890-95 that James began to suffer the psychic distress that made therapy necessary, and Edel's "retrospective method" (p. 17) included those years among the "treacherous" ones despite his subtitle "1895-1901."

12. Edel, *The Treacherous Years*, p. 155.

13. Matthiessen, *The James Family*, p. 509.

14. *The Treacherous Years*, p. 260.

15. Ibid., pp. 262, 264.

16. Frederick W. Dupee, ed., *Henry James: Autobiography* (New York: Criterion, 1956), p. 150. All subsequent references are to this edition and will appear in parentheses in the text. The original edition of the *Autobiography* is copyright 1913, 1914, and 1917 by Charles Scribner's Sons. All quotations are

reprinted here with the permission of the original publisher and Mr. Alexander R. James.

17. Quoted in ibid., p. viii.

18. Ibid., pp. ix, 263.

19. *The Sense of the Past* (New York: Scribner's, 1917), p. 49.

20. *Autobiography*, p. ix. Subsequent page numbers in parentheses in the text refer to this edition of the autobiography.

21. *The Untried Years*, p. 75.

22. A major discrepancy between James's life as recounted in the auto-biography and the historical record seems to have been intentional. When James was growing up, the family departed America for Europe in June 1855, stayed until the early summer of 1858, then returned to Europe again in October 1859, where they remained until September 1860. In *A Small Boy and Others*, James compressed these two trips into a single sojourn because, as reported by his nephew, he was "overcome" by the memory "of our poor father's impulsive journeyings to and fro and of the impression of aimless vacillation which the record might make upon the reader" (quoted in Edel, *The Untried Years*, p. 138).

23. *The Early Lectures of Ralph Waldo Emerson*, vol. 2, ed. Stephen E. Whicher et al. (Cambridge, Mass.: Harvard University Press, 1964), p. 4.

24. *Partial Portraits* (1888; rpt. London: Macmillan, 1919), pp. 388–89. "The Art of Fiction" originally appeared in *Longman's Magazine* for September 1884.

25. Emerson, *Early Lectures*, 2:44.

26. *Henry James: The Major Phase* (1944; rpt. New York: Galaxy, 1963), p. 32.

27. Edel, *The Untried Years*, p. 68.

28. *The Sense of the Past*, p. 49.

29. F. O. Matthiessen and Kenneth B. Murdock, eds., *The Notebooks of Henry James* (New York: Oxford Press, 1947), pp. 367–68.

6

The Next Generation

> "There are three times; a present of things past, a present of things present, and a present of things future." For these three do somehow exist in the soul, and otherwise I see them not: present of things past, memory; present of things present, sight; present of things future, expectation.—Saint Augustine, *Confessions*, 11:20

When Gertrude Stein left Radcliffe College in 1897, the teacher who had impressed her most indelibly (more even than George Santayana) was William James, at whose urging she entered the Johns Hopkins Medical School. The first published piece of writing of Gertrude Stein's exclusive authorship came directly out of her experience in James's and Hugo Münsterberg's laboratory at Harvard: "Cultivated Motor Automatism: A Study of Character in Its Relation to Attention" (*Psychological Review*, May 1898). "Attention" was no chance subject of inquiry for the fledgling psychological researcher because, in the language of the laboratory, it meant essentially the same thing as "consciousness"; and consciousness was the focal point of James's work at Harvard, as indeed it was of the work of most American psychologists in the 1890s. (Even the study of behavior in the mid-nineties, despite James's interest in habit, remained the province of ethics rather than psychology.)

Consciousness was also a chief preoccupation in that fiction to which a new generation of American writers had to accommodate themselves after about 1890 and to which Howells (with the work of Henry James especially in mind) gave the name "psychologism." For Gertrude Stein, Theodore Dreiser, Edith Wharton, Stephen Crane, Frank Norris, and Sherwood Anderson, the world within was not to be easily overlooked even by those among them who would come to concentrate, as literary naturalists, upon the world without. The new generation's reactions to the demands of psychological fiction covered the entire range of response—from frank imitation to outright revolt. It was, however, in the equally varied range of their autobiographical writing that members of the new generation faced the implications of modern consciousness psychology for their private lives as well as for their art.

The autobiographies to be discussed in the following pages illustrate this range. Despite its political radicalism, *The Autobiography of Lincoln Steffens* (1931) is artistically a conservative book. Steffens borrows traditional American motifs to construct a sequential story of personal advancement. His narrator can say of Russia under Lenin, "I have seen the future and it works," because Steffens's narrative assumes the linear configuration typical of the education form. Sherwood Anderson's *A Story Teller's Story* (1924) retains vestiges of a linear design in Anderson's account of his development as a writer, but this tendency must vie with an even stronger impulse toward the fluidity of modern psychological fiction. And in *The Autobiography of Alice B. Toklas* (1933) but especially in *Everybody's Autobiography* (1937), where linear development of character subsides into timeless being, Gertrude Stein adapted the premises of modern psychological fiction to autobiographical narrative with such rigor as to produce a mode of autobiography in which the education story was logically impossible.

Future Perfect: Lincoln Steffens

I

Written late in Steffens's career, the *Autobiography* was the culmination of a long search for an appropriate form. Ella Winter has described that search in a preface to a collection of her husband's essays and stories:

> He had been dogged by what he felt to be his inability to find a form to sum up, to express, all he had thought and felt as a result of his newspaper work and his many experiences. He came back to this plaint over and over in letters and in conversation. He knew you could not "tell it straight": either it would not be accepted or it would not be published.[1]

Steffens came back to this plaint in the *Autobiography* as well. The section entitled "Revolution" insists that muckraking in Europe gave "the killing sense that I could not write what I was finding out":

> How could one make a young, vigorous, optimistic people on a virgin, rich part of the earth's surface look ahead to those old peoples on old ground and see that the road we were on would lead up over the hill and down to Rome, Egypt, or China? How be heard saying that the process of political corruption we were reforming here and there was a mighty force that was, in Europe, making for the control of trade routes, spheres of influence, empire, war . . . ?[2]

But also, how could he say in 1914 that "the cost of war, economically and morally, would precipitate the revolution, which alone could change our course and our minds and save us" (p. 710)?

It is hard to know how much Steffens relied on hindsight for this account of what he thought in 1914. At the beginning of the war, he had not yet seen "the future"; and it was not until his return from Russia in March, 1919, that he could proclaim that the future "worked." But there can be little doubt that the *Autobiography* contains the essentials of Steffens's political philosophy as it stood in 1931, and in 1934 he summed up that philosophy in a single word: "It is Communism. For these United States. I mean *especially* for this great and successful country, at this very time of its distress and confusion. . . . "[3] To be sure, the *Autobiography* does not openly preach communism. The climate in which it was published and read was very different from the period of sunny prosperity in which it was written. Begun in 1925 and completed in the summer of 1930, much of the *Autobiography* was composed at a time when the prewar reformers and progressives had all but vanished. A muckraker's straightforward exposé was not likely to be heeded; and Steffens wanted to convince his audience, not to alienate them.

Steffens had used the autobiographical form on a small scale at least once before. At a meeting of the Jonathan Club of Los Angeles in 1907, he had tried to convince a group of prominent citizens that economic rather than moral forces govern human life. His argument, recounted in the *Autobiography*, took the form of "a narrative, my own story" (p. 572). After telling how he had gone forth believing that bad men caused bad government, Steffens explained his change of heart and concluded that the audience should seek to relieve those economic pressures that forced powerful men to "work against the greater, common welfare" (p. 573). Then he opened the floor to debate. A bishop in the audience finally asked the key question: "Who founded this system?" (p. 574). Steffens's reply, which he liked to repeat in later years, brings the long third section of the *Autobiography* to a climax:

> "Oh, I think I see," I said. "You want to fix the fault at the very start of things. Maybe we can, Bishop. Most people, you know, say it was Adam. But Adam, you remember, he said that it was Eve, the woman; she did it. And Eve said no, no, it wasn't she; it was the serpent. And that's where you clergy have stuck ever since. You blame the serpent, Satan. Now I come and I am trying to show you that it was, it is, the apple." (P. 574)

It is significant that Steffens's account of his life to the Jonathan Club should merge with this self-contained story of the Garden and the serpent, for the entire autobiography resembles the kind of writing to which Ella Winter referred in her preface. In "The Knowledge of Trees," "The Pines and the Borers," "The Light That Failed," and a number of similar tales written from 1922 to 1934, Steffens had experimented with fables in the Aesopian vein. According to Miss Winter, "Steffens chose the fable form to try and solve some of the contradictions of 'the typical problems that fretted all my life'; in this form he could be teaching, and teaching by implication, allegory, paradox, with humor and irony."[4]

The autobiographical form provided similar advantages. Steffens found in autobiography a means of telling it straight that would be acceptable to readers and publishers alike—by indirection. The form allowed him to escape the limitations of the short fable while maintaining the fabulist's essential narrative strategy. In *Moses in Red* (1926) Steffens had written an extended parable that dealt with the Exodus as a classic example of revolt, thereby making a traditional story patently revolutionary. The failure of that book to gain a hearing was still fresh in Steffens's mind when he got down to serious work on the *Autobiography* and may have influenced his conception of the new book. At any rate, Steffens took pains in the *Autobiography* to make a revolutionary story patently traditional. This reversal of strategy more than anything else accounted for Steffens's renewed favor with the reading public. The "special importance" of the *Autobiography*, as Granville Hicks saw it, lay in demonstrating "that there was a strictly American path to Communist conclusions."[5] Like Aesop before him, Steffens disguised his polemics by casting them in familiar, almost domestic, terms. The *Autobiography* succeeded where *Moses in Red* failed because it made "un-American" ideas seem blatantly American.

Hicks acknowledges that the *Autobiography* is "full of traditional American motifs," but his excellent essay deals primarily with Steffens's political views and, consequently, does not examine those motifs as narrative devices crucial to Steffens's art.[6] Indisputably a polemicist, Steffens was at least equally concerned to tell a good story. The propagandistic motive behind his narrative merges with the "creative, and therefore fictional, impulse" said by Northrop Frye to link autobiography with other forms of prose fiction. Steffens's American motifs, therefore, deserve careful attention because they provide the measure of his skill as a craftsman.

Steffens's persona adopts a variety of identities at different stages of his career, and in each case they are based on character types drawn from American popular literature, juvenile fiction, and folklore. The title figure of part 1, "A Boy on Horseback," comes out of the boy-book tradition established by Aldrich, Howells, and Mark Twain. (This section formed a major addition to the boy-book genre when *A Boy on Horseback* appeared as an independent volume in 1935.) A westernized Tom Sawyer or Huck Finn, Steffens's boy is mischievous, independent, and imaginative. He too sees "A-rabs" in every bush and gulch. Furthermore, his innocence is humorously threatened by the forces of civilization. Mrs. Neely, Steffens's childless friend, is another in a long line of well-meaning women who regard all boys as angelic savages to be reformed. Her civilizing influence carries Steffens to the brink of sissyhood and religion, as in this passage reminiscent of the machinations of an Aunt Polly or Sally Phelps:

> She put her arm around my neck and drew me into the parlor where she had all ready, on the sofa, a piled-up white bed. It looked good, all clean and cool, and I could have tumbled right into it myself, had she let me. But, no, she must undress me, put on me one of Mr. Neely's great nightgowns, and we kneeled together by the bed and prayed. (P. 76)

Since the boy on horseback is also drawn from the actual circumstances of Steffens's childhood in California, he has some advantages Tom Sawyer did not enjoy in Hannibal. Designed to inspire envy in eastern or midwestern boys and nostalgia in any adult reader who remembers his own childhood with affection, Steffens's boy is a true child of the Far West who, best of all, had the privilege of being educated by his horse: "I didn't know it then," Steffens recalls, "but I can see now, of course, that my father was using my horse to educate me, and he had an advantage over the school teachers; he was bringing me up to my own ideals; he was teaching me the things my heroes knew and I wanted to learn" (p. 26). The boy on horseback is by no means Steffens's only juvenile role. "I imagined myself," he says at one point, "as all sorts of persons . . . I fancied myself as the hero of every story I had read" (p. 27). By turns, Steffens's boy becomes a cowboy, trapper, statesman, and soldier. When he enters preparatory school at San Mateo, California, his father proposes a new hero. "To center my interest in the school he suggested that, besides Napoleon, I read *Tom Brown at Rugby*. That had some effect. As he expected, no doubt, I began to emulate Tom Brown" (p. 104). When preparatory school gives way to college, Steffens is offered still another model. A teacher inspires him to imitate the boy from the provinces, or young Ben Franklin, who is destined to make good:

> "Go to, boy. The world is yours. Nothing is done, nothing is known. The greatest poem isn't written, the best railroad isn't built yet, the perfect state hasn't been thought of. Everything remains to be done—right, everything." (P. 113)

As Steffens wades through Berkeley and on into the German universities, he continues to invent or borrow roles to play. When he returns from Europe having acted the part of the pseudo-sophisticated truth-seeker, Steffens recalls one of the roles denied him as a boy. At the beginning of "Seeing New York First," he receives a letter from his father, who, unaware that he is married, advises the prodigal to look for a job. Steffens tries, unsuccessfully:

> Here I was, what I had once grieved that I was not, a poor but willing young fellow, without parents, friends, or money, seeking a start in life, just a foothold on the first rung of the ladder: I would, like my boy heroes, attend to the rest. And I couldn't get the chance! I couldn't understand it. (P. 170)

This passage is intended to show Steffens's naïveté, but it also serves to prepare us for his subsequent rise. Part 2 of the

Autobiography is a mélange of conventions drawn from the American success story. Almost overnight Steffens becomes an established reporter, and at the end of the opening chapter he can write:

> In a word I was a success, and though I have never since had such a victory and have come to have some doubt of the success of success, I have never since failed to understand successful men; I know, as I see them, how they feel inside. (P. 178)

Daily advancing in his trade, Steffens goes on to make himself independent of it. He establishes important connections with public officials, including Police Commissioner Roosevelt. In chapter 15, he inherits "a fortune" from a German friend. And one chapter later he becomes "a capitalist": the inheritance "was only some $12,000, but I knew how to make it more. . . . I slowly, surely, easily made enough money to make me free for life, as my friend Johann Friedrich Krudewolf willed, free even of Wall Street" (p. 310).

After he has attained financial independence, Steffens does not cease "play-acting"; but he does settle on a single role. In section three of the *Autobiography*, his energies are concentrated on plying the muckrake or, rather, the lance, for Steffens invites comparison between the watchdog of public morality and the dazzling knight he had wanted to be as a child. Although Steffens emphasizes his skill at obtaining inside information from people in the know, he is careful to point up another side of the muckraker's quest. He is describing his former self when he says of a Pittsburgh businessman: he "had kept apart the child's picture of a noble world of brave men and good women, the picture of romance and the school histories" (p. 404). When Steffens "had discovered bit by bit what really went on in government and business," he too "had been first incredulous, then convinced, inspired like the heroes of old to go forth and fight, humbly, as a soldier under some great leader, the Monster of Corruption, Fraud, Lies" (p. 404).

The Quixotic strain in the muckraker's adventures recalls Steffens's description of himself as a young man at the end of "A Boy on Horseback." Returning from Europe in 1892 after completing most of the requirements for a degree in philosophy, Steffens did not know enough, he claimed, to realize that he was actually uneducated: "I was happily unaware that I was just a nice, original American boob, about to begin unlearning all my learning, and failing even at that" (p. 166). In such passages, the boy on horseback looks less like Tom Sawyer and more and more like Henry Adams. And, indeed, Steffens himself was probably aware of the likeness, for he had intended to call his finished autobiography "My Life of Unlearning."[7]

Whether or not Adams furnished a direct model for the *Autobiography*—and the chances are good that Steffens read Adams's book along with the thousands of other Americans who made the second edition a literary sensation—Steffens's basic theme is life conceived as a process of "de-education." Furthermore, many of the lessons Steffens had to unlearn were those Adams repudiated as holdovers from an eighteenth-century culture. By background and training, Steffens's mind was attuned to established American ideals, "the so-called New England ideals which came over from England to us with the Puritan, Pilgrim, and other fathers when they had moved west in search of land and liberty" (p. 473). These were the ideals of a "moral culture of right and wrong" (p. 492). When Steffens became shocked by the ignorance of his college professors, he was primarily concerned with *a priori* notions of proper behavior; and he left Berkeley to discover in European schools some solid basis for ethics, the study, as he defined it, of how life "ought" to be led (p. 151). Even after he returned from Europe and served his apprenticeship as a newspaper reporter in New York, Steffens continued to seek a ground for ethical beliefs. His search through the mire of political corruption was conducted, he says, with all the "taught ignorance" of his day (p. 375). Christened by Theodore Roosevelt with a name drawn from *The Pilgrim's*

Progress, the "muckraker" upheld the standard of militant morality that Henry Adams's grandfather had championed when he went forth into a world of evils to be destroyed.

Steffens's years in the academies were not totally without effect, however. The "German universities," he admitted, "had corrected my American culture to some extent" (p. 375). Here again Steffens's education paralleled Henry Adams's. If he got nothing else from his studies, he gleaned a generalized faith in the scientific method and the belief "that when there was a science of psychology, a science of sociology, and a science of biology, when we could know how man was born, bred, moved, and to what end, then we might lay out a program for the guidance of his conduct" (p. 164). Answers would come from science, and Steffens determined, as Adams had done, to bring the tools of scientific investigation out of the schoolroom into the world.

As a result of Steffens's dedication to science, the bulk of the *Autobiography*, including "Seeing New York First," "Muckraking," and "Revolution," is reminiscent of Henry Adams's frantic search for statistics and formulas that might explain his puzzling environment. Most of his life, as Steffens portrays it, is a fact-finding expedition in which the researcher continues to store up data against the day he will come to understand them. Consequently, the *Autobiography* has the over-all structure of a journey. The inveterate traveler cannot really begin his fictionalized life until he has a means of transportation. Only when he is given a pony can he say, "I had a world before me. I felt lifted up to another plane, with a wider range" (p. 26). When he outgrows both pony and horse, he moves on to the nomadic life of a student who ransacks five universities and returns home to admit, in effect, what Henry Adams dreaded to tell his father after his own student days: "Sir, I am a tourist!"[8] Nor does tourism end here. After "Seeing New York First," he *sees* most of America's major cities, Mexico, Europe, Russia, and the future. Toward the close of his life story, he sees America in a new light. (The last section of the *Autobiography* is entitled

"Seeing America at Last.") And all this "sight-seeing" (Steffens's phrase) ends in prophecy, a last excursion into the future. Almost to the end of his travels, Steffens insists that he is just a struggling student, an American boob who seeks to cast off moralistic preconceptions and plumb the depths of his own ignorance. It was this pose, so like Adams's pretense of ignorance and failure, that must have prompted Michael Gold to sneer at Steffens as a "cheeild" lost among the social battlefields.[9] But Gold apparently did not realize that Steffens's seeker, a figure familiar enough in American literature, merely represented a narrative stance. Steffens disarms us by parading forth his youthful persona's Americanism, and we forget that the experienced narrator is shrewd enough to capitalize on his earlier blunders. In the *Autobiography*, the role that subsumes all others is that of the traditional American innocent. The book is squarely within the tradition of *Innocents Abroad*, the supreme account of an American tourist whose misadventures provide the measure of a "smart" narrator's "educated intelligence." When Steffens's traveler becomes a fellow traveler late in the *Autobiography*, we (but especially the audience Steffens had in mind while in the late twenties) are prepared to accept anything he says. How question the confident, home-grown hero who establishes his sincerity by exposing his own weaknesses and who proves his wisdom by showing how he grew wise to all deceptions, including his own?

II

To label Steffens a "revolutionary" is to call attention to his undeniable sympathy with the Communist movement, but a strictly political application of the term falsifies Steffens's complex position. In the *Autobiography*, Steffens declared that Soviet Russia and the United States were heading toward the same socialistic destination by different routes. There are good reasons for suggesting that this proclamation was insincere, that Steffens really believed revolution to be necessary or, at least, desirable. But Steffens himself did not become an active revolutionary. As Ella Winter has said, he could never bring himself to "organizationally join the revolutionaries who expected to lead a new society."[10] Although he could justify the terror tactics of the Bolsheviks, Steffens remained personally ambivalent toward their regime. In a letter commenting on *Moses in Red*, Steffens explained that Jehovah would have to dispose of reformers like himself "to save mankind, because we also were reared—in opposition, but none the less—in Egypt."[11] No wonder Steffens experienced the sense of contradiction of which Ella Winter once spoke. Justin Kaplan's recent biography of Steffens has this to say about the new Moses: "Looking for absolution from history, Steffens succeeded only in coming up with desperate answers, fevered optimism, and a ticlike string of paradoxes." Like the old Moses, he "was able to recognize salvation but was beyond being saved."[12]

The radicalism that Steffens openly advocates in the *Autobiography* is not so much political as philosophical, a revolution in thought. Steffens wanted to teach his readers to "see" in a new light. This, of course, was what Thoreau had wanted; and, in fact, Steffens was much closer to Thoreau's way of thinking than he realized. Having begun adult life as a philosophical idealist, Steffens thought he had become a convert to empiricism. By defending the scientific attitude, he convinced himself that he had achieved a measure of genuine objectivity. He had turned to science as a corrective to inherited ways of thinking (the old "ideals" of England and New England), and from Wilhelm Wundt's lectures in Germany he had learned the value of "facts, nothing but facts": "The laboratory where we sought the facts and measured them by machinery was a graveyard where the old idealism walked as a dreadful ghost and philosophical thinking was a sin" (p. 149). The doctrine Steffens came to preach— and he described it as "revolutionary"—was: "No more thinking; no more right thinking; no more believing or logical reasoning from premises to conclusions" (p. 851). When the new doctrine became law, it would usher in a new order: "Wondering would supplant convictions, insight inspiration; experiment would blow up argument; and as for our conclusions, they would not be uplifted into principles and creeds but tried out as . . . working hypotheses" (pp. 851–52).

Steffens failed to practice his own preachments, however. In actuality, the science intended as an antidote to Steffens's moralism fed his originally undisguised tendency to think in absolute terms. Late in the *Autobiography*, he finds evidence that the spirit of science has invaded American business: "Big business was absorbing science, the scientific attitude and the scientific method. Cocksureness, unconscious ignorance, were giving way to experiment . . . " (p. 851). "This," Steffens writes, "is revolutionary":

> If this spirit had got out of the science laboratories into business in a business country, it would seal the doom of our old Greek-Christian culture. It would spill over into politics, economics, life. . . . A new, the new, culture was sweeping down over us, and big business, and the old root of all evil! (Pp. 851–52)

Belying Steffens's claim to detachment and objectivity, the evangelical tone of this passage suggests that Steffens had found a new religion to replace the old. Despite his resemblance to Henry Adams, Steffens pushed his education across a limit Adams never approached. In communism, Steffens believed he had found a positive program whereby order could be imposed on chaos. The dialectical materialism of the Communist party became his personal philosophy, and Steffens could scientifically justify the misapplication of science that had led him to it: "My old German professor of psychology had taught us to distinguish between perception and apperception, between seeing things with the eyes and reaching out with the mind to grasp them, what the new school of *Gestalt* psychology now calls 'insight' " (p. 492).

Steffens the political radical, then, had been doubly conservative in his *Autobiography*. Not only had he adopted for his life story the education form by which members of the preceding literary generation sought continuity in their own life-journeys; in bringing his traveler safely to Altruria and then inviting others to follow, he harked back a generation further to the shores of Walden Pond. Steffens's peculiar form of insight was closer to the "intuition" of the transcendentalists than to the induction of the experimental psychologists. In embracing the materialism of Marx and Engels, whose method extended back to Hegel and beyond Hegel to Plato, Steffens had circled around to a position approximating his early idealism. For dialectical materialism posted, in Emerson's terms, a final source beyond which analysis (or, rather, synthesis) could not go. Sight-seeing had led Steffens, as it had led the transcendentalists, to a vision of the absolute. Steffens's *Autobiography*, in which the author's journey through life is a metaphor for the American traveler's movement toward truth, allowed him to develop his own version of the doctrine of correspondence. No matter that Steffens's dialectic was necessarily different from Emerson's or that his philosophy dispensed with any transcendent dimension. The transcendentalist obtained the higher Truth by a series of ascensions taking him out of the material world, and the dialectical materialist reached truth by a series of reductions. But if the materialist sought the lowest common denominator of human life rather than the highest, it was nonetheless *common*—even universal. Wundt's old psychology student had written another story of the American seer "En-Masse," and Steffens's personal narrative of education had been swallowed up in another of his political or philosophical allegories.

Then as Now: Sherwood Anderson

Like Mark Twain, with whom he often identified, Sherwood Anderson never wandered far from autobiography. There is something of Anderson in Sam of *Windy McPherson's Son* (1916), in George Willard of *Winesburg, Ohio* (1919), in Hugh

McVey of *Poor White* (1921); there is an even more direct connection, if possible, between Tar Moorehead and the author of
Tar: A Midwest Childhood (1926). But it was in two widely
separated volumes, *A Story Teller's Story* (1924) and his posthumous *Memoirs* (1942), that a supreme maker of personal
legend and myth professed to drop the mask of fiction he once
said he needed in order to "face" himself and "accept" himself.[13]
Of these two books—the *Memoirs* was never really finished—
A Story Teller's Story is the more enduring and comes nearer to
demonstrating the relationship in all Anderson's work between
fact and the more "essential" truth of what he called "fancy,"
the truth of legend.

I

Although Anderson declared that "the true history of life is
but a history of moments," those moments in *A Story Teller's
Story* are part of a continuum.[14] We betray the book if we forget
that it is the "writer's journey through his own imaginative world
and through the world of facts" promised by the epigraph. As
Anderson retrieves his precious moments through time, the
narrative takes on a linear movement that marks it unmistakably
as a narrative of education. He is telling the story, Anderson can
say near the close of book 4, of "my own imaginative life in
America" (p. 407). Like Henry James, Anderson recognized that
he had written the history of an artist's development, and that
"journey" unfolded in a number of progressive stages.

Book 1 is a tale of birth in a work as rife with images of
procreation as Whitman's "Song of Myself." In the opening
chapter, Anderson and his brothers are old enough to have read
James Fenimore Cooper and to imagine themselves as La
Longue Carabine and Le Cerf Agile in a wonderful re-creation of
boyhood fantasy that Gertrude Stein called "almost the best
piece of writing I know."[15] But through a Shandian maneuver,
Anderson postpones his physical birth until "Note" 9. ("Notes"
was the term Anderson used instead of "chapters" for the small-

er divisions of his book.) This maneuver releases Anderson from the orthodox, and sometimes mechanical, practice of describing his parents from the viewpoint of an adult narrator. Anderson wants to give a child's perspective of them and, with a child's license, recalls an impoverished father reduced from the harness business to house and sign painting. He is a romantic southerner who cannot stay still long enough to provide for the large family he is always temporarily deserting; but Anderson's father is a born storyteller, and he charms the faintly disapproving son who will inherit his talent. Anderson's mother, on the other hand, is portrayed as loving, silent, once beautiful and soon dead. She is the family provider, and she brings a trace of mystery to the line with her Italian blood from a shadowy grandmother whose main feature is a single, hate-filled eye. Once he has established these figures, Anderson is ready to introduce himself.

The narrator's chief reason for postponing the moment of his birth, however, is suggested by the remark, attributed to Joseph Conrad near the end of the book, "that a writer only began to live after he began to write" (p. 399). By this logic, Anderson is "but ten years old" when the narrative closes in 1923, his forty-seventh year on another scale (p. 399). By similar logic, the man of imagination is not born until his imagination begins to function, so Anderson's physical birth is immediately preceded by a more formative event. Soon to be pulled from the womb in chapter 9, Anderson is taken by his father in chapter 8 to a farm where there is a new house to paint. The father tells his employer a wild tale about his descent from an old New England family. The boy hears everything from a hayloft, where he burrows sleepily into the enveloping warmth (this particular womb is somewhat crowded since the farmer's fat son is also asleep in it): "At that moment as I lay deeply buried in the warm hay and when the fancy of my own flesh-and-blood father, down on the floor of the barn, was giving me a birthright of decaying Germanic gentlefolk the dark old woman who was my grandmother was more in my line" (p. 102).

Viewed as an "education," *A Story Teller's Story* is a writer's account of his quest for his birthright, and that quest begins when the boy imagines a father more to his liking. Lying deep in the hay, he conceives of a dark, cruel though handsome smuggler who is cast ashore on a southern beach. The smuggler marries a beautiful revolutionary with the face of Anderson's real mother, and she gives birth to him in a fisherman's hut. Soon after, the father sacks a South American city and deserts his virtuous wife for a younger woman. "And if you have read Freud," says Anderson, "you will find it of additional interest that, in my fanciful birth, I have retained the very form and substance of my earthly mother while getting an entirely new father . . . only to sling mud at him. I am giving myself away to the initiated, that is certain" (p. 114). This is Anderson's fanciful birth; it is also, as he says, the boy's "birth into the world of fancy" (p. 114). The imaginary history of his imagined father was young Anderson's "first invented tale" (p. 102). Having brought him to life in the world of the fancy, book 1 carries him to the end of boyhood.

Book 2 records the storyteller's adolescence and young manhood through 1898–99, Anderson's year of army service during the Spanish-American War. If the first book recounts the birth of the artist's imagination, the second tells of its undisciplined growth and frustration. Early in this section, Anderson has a vision of himself in a vacant lot at the head of a well-ordered army. He has already equated words with soldiers at his command, so the vision is a dream of both the power and the order the storyteller can hope to win through his art. Confusing the power of his imagination with sexual potency, Anderson's younger self must protect his vision from less imaginative, ordinary beings, especially other young men. He is aided in this task by Nora, a working girl who resembles his mother and whose forbearance enables him to nurse his vision. When his potency is put to the test in a fight with an "athlete" who has become a "symbol" to him, Anderson is defeated; he breaks off with Nora and resolves on a different life from the life of the imagination that has failed to hold sway over actuality: "I will become a man of action, in the mood of the American of my day. I will build railroads, conquer empires, become rich and powerful" (p. 218).

This new dream, of course, proves to be even more ineffectual than the old one. Citing Mark Twain's characterization of life as "just a great machine," Henry Adams's love of lost medieval craftsmanship, and the powerful influence of Henry Ford, Anderson presents his younger self as an unsuspecting victim of standardization in the industrial age. Yet his imagination refuses to be suppressed. He tempers the worldly cynicism taught him by a Judge Turner when his imagination sets to work on the frail, dying Alonzo Berners. He imagines Berners to be a paragon of sympathy, the kind of power the incipient storyteller will have to develop if he is to acquire an artist's receptivity to experience. At the end of book 2, however, the leader of visionary armies is swallowed up in the real army's anonymous mass.

The place of book 3 in the storyteller's development is defined by its two climactic moments. When the storyteller strides "out of the door of buying and selling," he leaves behind the "long and tangled phase" he had misguidedly entered in book 2 (p. 313). Forgetting his vociferations against heroes of romance with their sudden, implausible changes of heart, Anderson follows a long-standing cliché of success literature by giving his life a turning point: from this moment on, his hero will dedicate himself to storytelling and the life of the imagination. Having given up a life of affairs, he has finally found his true vocation.

The second moment merely confirms him in this decision; the storyteller cannot go back to his former life, but he does not want to. The blind night watchman at the factory he once managed fails to lay hands on the returning snooper because Anderson has sailed far ahead and out of the darkness enveloping both the factory and the "watchman." Confirmed in his calling, he has not, however, learned his trade. "What I wanted most," Anderson says, "was the men who would help me solve certain

problems connected with the craft to which I was devoted. Could
I find such fellows? Would they do it?" (p. 367).

Anderson could, and they did. The last leg of his journey, book
4, takes Anderson to New York, later Europe, and the tutelage
of Van Wyck Brooks, Waldo Frank, Paul Rosenfeld, Alfred
Stieglitz (to whom *A Story Teller's Story* is dedicated), Gertrude Stein, and others. It is a grateful tribute to many of the
gifted men and women whose influence guided a fellow writer
coming late to his craft. But in thanking the non-midwesterners
who encouraged him, Anderson underplayed the influence of
those midwestern writers who together represented the Chicago
renaissance of which Anderson was a part. The author of *A Story
Teller's Story* clearly intended his personal journey to reverber-
ate with that tradition of American literary pilgrimages best
exemplified in Howells's *Literary Friends and Acquaintance*
and in one interpretation of Mark Twain's career; here was
another midwesterner come East to be educated: "I was a
middle-westerner trying to pick up cultural scraps in New York,
trying to go to school there" (p. 393). Most midwesterners
thought of New York as the place where culture was to be
"breathed in," says Anderson. "Mark Twain thought he would
find it in Boston—a whole generation of Americans thought that"
(p. 365).

If the life of a new pilgrim from Clyde, Ohio, held true to
form, Anderson could expect his readers to anticipate, he would
not remain a schoolboy for long. Soon the apprentice storyteller
and student of the American East graduates to Europe ("the
old home of the crafts"), where book 4 leaves Anderson ruminat-
ing before the cathedral at Chartres: "In the end I had become
a teller of tales." "I liked my job." (Pp. 390, 409.) It is, however,
in the epilogue—far from "superfluous," as one critic has called
it—that Anderson reaches maturity as an artist.[16] The seemingly
irrelevant exchange with an unnamed author of football stories
who is vaguely aware that his talent has been stunted is more
than another of the tongue-lashings Anderson reserved for

formula writers and romancers corrupted by public taste. It shows Anderson in a role he has sought to fulfill throughout the autobiography.

In *A Story Teller's Story*, Anderson's discovery and exercise of his birthright as an artist cannot be separated from his search for an acceptable father. The quest begins with Irwin Anderson, redrawn here more sympathetically than his counterparts in his son's earlier work. No longer the windy ne'er-do-well who fathered Sam McPherson, the senior Anderson is honored for his skill as a raconteur; and the future writer twice repeats the refrain of one of his father's songs, "You grow more like your dad every day" (p. 75). This version of Irwin Anderson is replaced in his son's narrative by the handsome smuggler; by Judge Turner, who helped "educate" young Anderson "in the ways of the world"; by the patriarchs of American business whose examples inspired Anderson to dream of owning a factory that would feed and house its workers like children; and by the unknown author of an old Norse Saga about Fredis (p. 157). When Anderson discovers this last, best father (at the exact point in the narrative when he accepts his vocation), he has discovered his proper identity. The storyteller's search for his birthright has led to the conclusion that he must be his own father, that he must, in effect, generate himself in his own image of what a teller of tales should be; and his life story cannot be cut off until he fully assumes that parental role. Hence the necessity of the epilogue. Anderson is there cloaked in the authority of one who has mastered his craft and whose wisdom is sought after by such "youngsters" as the writer of football fiction. He has at last become the patriarch he dreamed of being in an earlier life.

II

In December 1918, Anderson wrote to Van Wyck Brooks: "I have been reading *The Education of Henry Adams* and feel tremendously its importance as a piece of American writing."[17] Anderson was to read, reread, and thoroughly digest the *Edu-*

cation during the coming years. In 1932, he put Adams (along with Jefferson, Lincoln, Whitman, and Emerson) on his personal list of the five greatest Americans.[18] In 1936, he explained that he was attending a national American Federation of Labor convention "for education." "It may be, as Henry Adams seemed to think, that there is nothing else to be got, a little education."[19] And Anderson's posthumous *Memoirs* showed, as James Schevill has said, that a "major theme of both writers was the suppression of creative imagination by the material forces of American society."[20] It was, however, *A Story Teller's Story*—written when Anderson's first impressions of the *Education* were still relatively fresh—that best showed both what Anderson learned from Henry Adams and where he fixed the limits of his agreement with the quintessential New Englander. *A Story Teller's Story* may be read as a midwesterner's answer to the *Education*, a sequel and modification in which Anderson assumed the role of the New American whom Adams called for but claimed not to have found.

One basis of Adams's appeal for Anderson seems to have been his recognition of the power of sex. *A Story Teller's Story* quotes at length that portion of chapter 25 of the *Education* associating the Virgin with Venus and concluding, "An American Virgin would never dare command; an American Venus would never dare exist" (p. 379).[21] In such passages, Adams confirmed Anderson's suspicion that Puritanism had warped the American's sexuality by forcing upon him a heritage of sexual repression, the repression of all forms of instinctual behavior, in fact. The dissociation of intellect and emotion, morality and desire, head and hand left the American, as Anderson understood his plight, in a divided state of the sort that the *Education* had documented to the last detail: "To the imaginative man in the modern world," said Anderson, "something becomes, from the first, sharply defined. Life splits itself into two sections and, no matter how long one may live or where one may live, the two ends continue to dangle, fluttering about in the empty air"

(p. 77). Anderson's names for these sections were "the life of fancy" and the life of "fact" (p. 77). As a man of imagination, he felt the strong attraction of the fancy, and at times gave in to it so completely that the narrator of *A Story Teller's Story* becomes like the boy in the hayloft who was "beginning to re- make his own life more to his own liking by plunging into a fanciful life" (p. 123). The "problem" according to Anderson— and he might have been speaking also for the author of both *Mont-Saint-Michel and Chartres* and *The Life of George Cabot Lodge*—"is to reach down through all the broken surface dis- tractions of modern life to that old love of craft out of which cul- ture springs" (p. 81).

The problem belonged most acutely to the American artist. This was a slightly submerged theme in the *Education*; it was an overt one in Adams's *Life of Lodge*; it was the only theme, by Anderson's account, in the work of his one-time friend and mentor Van Wyck Brooks. The same letter in which Anderson mentioned his reading of the *Education* named another book that greatly influenced him and whose title must have seemed directed personally to a young writer seeking artistic maturity. The theme of *America's Coming-of-Age* (1915) and of all Brooks's criticism as Anderson paraphrased it was "that a man cannot be an artist in America" (p. 394). What happened to "Twain, Howells, Whitman, Poe and the New Englanders," Anderson interpreted Brooks to say, was that "they had the rotten luck to be born in a new land" (p. 393). Coming at a time when Anderson was trying to get a perspective upon his coun- try's literature, Brooks helped Anderson to his own version of the old complaint about America's barren climate for art. Ameri- ca lacked "culture," Anderson said, because her whole energy had been diverted into providing the material needs of a new country that was growing at a tremendous rate. The conse- quence for the artist was what it had been for Irwin Anderson, the original American storyteller:

My father lived in a land and in a time when what one later begins to understand a little as the artist in man could not by any possibility be understood by his fellows. Dreams then were to be expressed in building railroads and factories, in boring gas wells, stringing telegraph poles. There was room for no other dream and since father could not do any of these things he was an outlaw in his community. (P. 26)

This is the twentieth-century notion of the artist as pariah, and, in expressing it, Anderson showed himself to belong to a later literary generation than the one that fascinated Van Wyck Brooks. But it also describes the artist's dilemma in terms that indicated where *A Story Teller's Story* departed from the *Education*. The materialism paralyzing the artist in America was not, as Anderson interpreted it, the love of money for its own sake. Few aliens paid as little attention as Americans did to how their money was spent. The American disease was the press and drive to be up and doing, the wanderlust and restlessness that were making expatriates of a "generation" of American writers at the time Anderson was composing his autobiography. The man who had been shifted from pillar to post as a child, who spent much of his adult life in hotel rooms, and whose autobiography reconstructed his life as a search for patrimony and a home, was well qualified to diagnose his needs and those of the culture he represented:

I wanted, as all men do, to belong.
To what? To an America alive, an America that was no longer a despised cultural foster child of Europe, with unpleasant questions always being asked about its parentage, to an America that had begun to be conscious of itself as a living home-making folk, to an America that had at last given up the notion that anything worth while could ever be got by being in a hurry. . . . (P. 395)

In *A Story Teller's Story* Anderson professed to believe that the transformation had already taken place. He arranged in the final book to leave an impression of cultural ferment by calling attention to the spirit of Greenwich Village, to such periodicals as the *Masses*, the *Seven Arts*, the *New Republic*, and the *Nation*, and to those writers and intellectuals who contributed to the midwestern pilgrim's education. He arranged to show himself at home in that ferment and even to show its superiority to European culture in the final chapter of book 4.

Like Henry Adams, Anderson in this chapter sits before Chartres contemplating the motives of the workmen who toiled there. But instead of attributing their devotion to a lost instinct, he proclaims the spirit of their craftsmanship to be alive still: "Always wood for carvers to carve, always little flashing things to stir the souls of painters, always the tangle of human lives for the tale-tellers to mull over, dream over . . ." (p. 401). And instead of forgetting the present in thoughts of twelfth-century France, Anderson's imagination turns upon twentieth-century America. He makes the entrance to Chartres the scene of a little American drama by recalling an American tourist who pauses there to cry and compose herself before rejoining her husband (or lover) and the French woman who is stealing him from her. Then Anderson speaks his mind and that of the fellow American, Paul Rosenfeld, who sits beside him: "We would both soon be going back to America to our separate places there. We wanted to go, wanted to take our chances of getting what we could out of our own lives in our own places. We did not want to spend our lives living in the past, dreaming over the dead past of a Europe from which we were separated by a wide ocean. Americans with cultural impulses had done too much of that sort of thing in the past" (p. 407).

Anderson admits that this moment of confidence is only a "mood" (p. 409). *A Story Teller's Story* is often as critical of American life as Adams's *Education* could be, and Anderson more than once tempers his optimism and sentimentality with the irony of "an American Falstaff kind of laugh" that sweeps away all pretension (p. 325). But Anderson will not accept the ostensible lesson of *The Education of Henry Adams*—that the new

conditions have brought about vast new problems in accultura-
tion without providing the means for solving them. "The future
of the western world lay with America," Anderson is able to
say. "Everyone knew that. In Europe they knew it better than
they did in America" (pp. 407–8). Reminding his audience of
the ending of *Poor White*, a novel about the onset of the dynamo
and the factory, Anderson compares the writer's tales with the
colored stones his hero picked up on the beach of Sandusky,
Ohio. They are permanent and beautiful, and they represent the
end of a time of homeless wandering. In an act of faith that
Henry Adams would have found naïve, Anderson affirmed the
power of the storyteller's imagination to create lasting moments
in a present to which the past is always accessible.

III

It was Anderson's narrative treatment of those "moments,"
in fact, that most sharply divided his kind of autobiography from
that of Adams's generation while linking it with the autobiographies of Gertrude Stein and Proust. Near the end of book 1 of
A Story Teller's Story, Anderson writes: "Those of my critics
who declare I have no feeling for form will be filled with delight
over the meandering formlessness of these notes" (p. 123).
This was Anderson's challenge to those immature and typically
American critics, as he considered them, who insisted that every
narrative should have a plot in the Aristotelian sense of a logically interrelated sequence of actions. *A Story Teller's Story*
has a traditional plot, as we have seen. But plot in Anderson's
narrative finally loses primacy to "form," "an altogether more
elusive and difficult thing to come at" (p. 352). The overriding
form of *A Story Teller's Story* resembles not only that of *Re-
membrance of Things Past* but the methodless method of *Mark
Twain's Autobiography*.

Although he does not ignore chronology, Anderson ranges
freely back and forth between his personal past and the present time at which he writes. Here, for example, is a passage

from the "Epilogue." The speaker has just parted from his friend
Edward; earlier in a restaurant they together had watched a fur-
tive man whom they imagined to be an ex-convict, and Anderson's narrator has returned to his hotel room, where he is visited
by another stranger:

> What I mean is that my mind again did a thing it is always doing.
> It leaped away from the man sitting before me, confused him with
> the figures of other men. After I had left Edward I had walked
> about thinking my own thoughts. Shall I be able to explain what
> happened at that moment? In one instant I was thinking of the
> man now sitting before me and who had wanted to pay me this
> visit, of the ex-thief seen in the restaurant, of myself and my friend
> Edward, and of the old workman who used to come and stand at
> the kitchen door to talk with mother when I was a boy.
> Thoughts went through my mind like voices talking. (P. 419)

This is close to the free association that took Clemens's autobiographical dictations wherever the impulse of the moment led
him, and Anderson admits at one point that he is writing a
record of the "vagrant thoughts, hopes, ideas" that have
"floated" through his mind (p. 100).

What distinguishes Anderson's method from Clemens's and
gives *A Story Teller's Story* a unity and control lacking in *Mark
Twain's Autobiography*, however, is a somewhat different set
of assumptions about the nature of memory and the past.
Whereas Clemens came to fear that the America of his boyhood
was irrevocably lost and lamented the gulf between past and
present by writing a narrative dissociating the two, Anderson
in hopeful moments assumed that the past could be regained
through the power of the artist's retrospective imagination. Although Anderson felt a closer kinship with Clemens, who, according to Anderson, struggled unsuccessfully to keep his
"proud, conscious innocence" in an age of disillusionment, the
narrator of *A Story Teller's Story* sometimes sounds more like
that invincible innocent Walt Whitman:[22]

Aha! You do not know, but I do. You wait now, I shall tell you.
I have felt all, everything. . . .
Do I not know? While I walked in the street there were such
words came, in ordered array! I tell you what—words have color,
smell; one may sometimes feel them with the fingers as one touches
the cheek of a child. (P. 291)

When the narrator of *A Story Teller's Story* is chanting in
this key, he attributes to words not only a palpable reality but
the kind of creative power vested in language by the American
Adam whom Whitman is said to have incarnated. In such moods,
self-expression—the outlet denied to so many of Anderson's
blighted characters—becomes for him as for the transcendentalists
one with action, with creation even; and Anderson can renew
contact with the past because he remakes it by naming the
images that float into his consciousness. Through "the in-
strumentality of these little words" he should be able, Anderson
tells us, "to give you the very smell of the little street wherein
I just walked," to make "you feel just the way the evening light
fell over the faces of the houses and the people" (p. 291).[23]

He should have this power, but the storyteller is often unequal
to his task. The storyteller's business as Anderson sometimes
defines it is to express the ineffable hidden lives of the men and
women he has known. "Will he accomplish his purpose? It is
sure he will not" (p. 296). Only rarely can the storyteller generate forms ("just the words and the arrangement of words") to
fit his raw material. This is why *A Story Teller's Story* is
constructed both as a story of education and as a record of
"moments"—the moment before bedtime when Anderson's mother rubbed warm animal fat on the chapped hands of her sons,
the moment when a small-town judge dropped his guard of
smiling cynicism, the moment when young Anderson learned
from an invalid to "live in another, suffer in another, love another
perhaps" (p. 260).

If, however, they resemble moments of the sort of illumination that Emerson and Whitman prolonged into steady vision, their very infrequency should warn us that Anderson could not ultimately make of himself the transcendentalist he sometimes wanted to be. For Anderson in the twentieth century, "there was no God in the sky, no God in myself, no conviction in myself that I had the power to believe in a God . . . " (p. 270). Furthermore, Anderson was too much the heir of the realists to leave the commonplace world behind in his flights of fancy. Like a disciple of Howells, he scolds the popular romancer who has "separated himself from actual life" (p. 354). Having lost touch with ordinary experience, he has become "irrevocably dead": "The actuality of life could not reach him. On all sides of him people suffered, were touched with moments of nameless joy, loved and died, and the manufacturer of society detectives, desert heroes and daring adventures by sea and land could no longer see life at all" (p. 354). Anderson's storyteller would not separate himself from "life," and his characteristic post at a window looking down on a city street or country road suggests an affinity with the gentlemen who look down from their windows in Henry James's house of fiction. For Anderson, too, art resulted from the responsive perceiver's appropriation of the unappropriated object. The storyteller never lost sight of that object even though his imagination (or "fancy") lent it forms the object did not possess in real life.

Yet Anderson's moments are not exactly those of the realist either. With a respect for actuality inherited from realism and with a faith in the creative power of the imagination that recalls a still earlier literary generation, Anderson records moments similar to the epiphanies of modern psychological fiction. The storyteller's technique of prolonging his moments by drawing them out in the telling is not unlike the psychological duration that replaces "mechanical" time in some stories by Virginia Woolf, Katherine Mansfield, and Gertrude Stein, from the last of whom Anderson may have heard about Bergsonian time and the Frenchman's theory of memory. A good example is the pivotal book 3, recalling perhaps the most famous moment in Anderson's career.

"What I am trying to do," Anderson says of book 3, "is to give the processes of my own mind at two distinct moments of my own life" (p 301). Although they really cannot be separated, the "first" moment is the instance (so Anderson chose to remember it) when he walked out of the Anderson Manufacturing Company, Elyria, Ohio, and left the world of business behind. Glossing over the several months the process of separation actually required in 1912–13, Anderson recalls looking into his secretary's eyes, laughing gayly, and saying, "I have been wading in a long river and my feet are wet" (p. 313). Then, in a one-sentence paragraph, comes the almost anticlimactic break: "Again I laughed as I walked lightly toward the door and out of a long and tangled phase of my life, out of the door of buying and selling, out of the door of affairs" (p. 313). Superimposed on the moment of separation from his life of action is a second moment two years later when by night Anderson revisits Elyria "to spend an evening alone with myself in the midst of the shadows of a former life" (p. 315). After slipping unseen past a banker to whom he owes money and plunging into the darkness along a railroad track, Anderson's narrator recalls coming upon his old factory; his name has been removed from the building, and a new name is in its place. But he is not given long to contemplate the loss of an old identity because the half-blind night watchman who earlier interrupted Anderson's dreams of a patriarchal business empire comes out of the door and lunges at him. Pretending to be drunk, the narrator staggers away, singing a song his father taught him about a ship that never returned.

When they arrive, Anderson's two distinct moments come as flashes of insight and decision, as epiphanies almost. In the meantime, however, his narrator has consumed an entire short book. He has anticipated them half a dozen times, and each

time he has drifted away before finally bringing the two moments to completion. At the beginning of "Note 2," for example,
he writes:

> One morning I had left . . . my poor little factory, like an illegiti-
> mate child, on another man's doorstep. I had left, merely taking
> what money was in my pocket, some eight or ten dollars.
>   What a moment that leaving had been! To one of the European
> artists I afterward came to know the situation would have been un-
> believably grotesque. (P. 298)

And the narrator is off on one of his ruminations, this time about
the function of money in American as opposed to European
society. He ruminates at other times on the American's typical
mixture of northern morality and southern warmth, on the artist's plight in America (an important preoccupation in the autobiography), on the wanderlust and rootlessness of American life.
Moreover, the storyteller suspends his account of the two
climactic moments to recall additional moments in his past that
bear upon them. He remembers a Sunday afternoon in childhood
when he spied on an old carpenter who stroked the trunk of a
tree with a craftsman's sensuous pleasure in the feel of his materials. He remembers sitting with the materials of his own
trade, clean white sheets of paper, ranged before him and thinking about a life consecrated to art. He remembers a man and
his wife arguing in a potato patch. In one reverie that almost
grows into a typical Anderson tale, he further remembers a meeting in a Chicago advertising agency with clients who want to
sell plows. One of the men has a scar beneath his beard, and the
scar brings to life an old memory or "story" the narrator has
never told (p. 335). His mind wanders from the room, and he recalls lying down to sleep in a field outside an Indiana town
where he was once forced off a freight train. The narrator
awakes to find two brothers fighting a third man in the field.
He is their sister's lover, and she lies partly undressed at their
feet:

And now one of them had got a knife out of his pocket and had slashed at the lover, laying his cheek open, and they might have killed the man as the woman and I watched trembling but at that moment he got away and ran across the field toward his own house followed by the others. (P. 338)

The men return, having reached an understanding; they have brought a preacher and there is a marriage ceremony. Then Anderson's narrator returns to the advertising office where he imagines the man with the scar to be the injured lover of long ago:

And now in fancy the bearded man and I were walking and talking together and I was telling him of the scene in the field and of what I had seen and he had told me of what I had not seen. (P. 341)

Book 3 ends with the narrator's imaginative re-creation of the lovers' wedding night. They did not undress, he imagines the bearded man to say; they lay together all night "holding fast to each other's hands" (p. 343).

When precisely does this last "moment" take place? It is narrated in the past tense; but since the events described by the bearded man never occurred, it can hardly be located in Anderson's youth or early manhood. And since the conversation with the bearded man did not occur either, the moment really cannot be set in a Chicago advertising agency some time after Anderson's departure from Elyria in 1913. The act of imagining the conversation may have taken place then; but did it follow even remotely the same sequence Anderson reports? Clearly the language and probably the order of Anderson's reverie are the work of the storyteller at the time he composes his narrative, so the "memory" of the lovers' wedding night is really a composite of at least three widely spaced moments; it is an accretion of forms in the autobiographer's consciousness roughly analogous to the exposure of three different images on the same photographic plate. And much the same may be said of all the moments in book 3. They blend with each other, with the remembered or imagined moments of their occurrence, and with the moment of telling. The past as the autobiographer draws upon it is the sum total of the interlocking images of past experience stored in his memory over a long period of time.

Whether or not Anderson's moments owe anything to Henri Bergson (and Anderson's emphasis on sensation and intuition further suggests a kinship), they partake of the general modernist tendency, of which Bergson's philosophy was one expression, to portray life by internal time rather than by essence. (Another such expression of that tendency was William James's idea that consciousness is continuous and that identity resides in that continuity.) Short of making Anderson out to be another Proust, it is still accurate to see *A Story Teller's Story* as the product of a memory that recaptured the past in a way denied to Mark Twain, Howells, and even Henry James.

For Anderson, the past is not something that must be lost to an uncongenial present or something in which an intruder from the present can become lost like the hero of *The Sense of the Past*. Nor does he deny all distinctions between past and present as the transcendentalists often did. Rather, Anderson's narrator can make himself present in the past because the past subsists in his present consciousness. The past for him revives as memory and fancy call it to life at any given moment. The same holds true for events in even the very remote past. In book 3, having quoted from the old Norse epic in which Fredis, sister of Eric, murders two brothers, Anderson re-creates in American slang the thoughts and words of "the unknown writer" whose storytelling has moved him (p. 330). "Well," says Anderson, "there was my father, there was myself" (p. 332).

The Continuous Present: Gertrude Stein

Gertrude Stein was hardly unknown when she published *The Autobiography of Alice B. Toklas* in 1933. "She had a reputation, several of them," as Richard Bridgman has said.[24] But the success of the best-selling *Autobiography* came as a shock. She was temporarily unable to write, and she developed a fixation upon the question of identity. "It was then," says the author of *Everybody's Autobiography*, "I began to think about am I I because my little dog knows me."[25] Gertrude Stein's not altogether satisfactory explanation was that the self-questioning came when she acquired a large popular following. "All of a sudden I was not just I because so many people did know me," she told the readers of *Vanity Fair* just before the start of her triumphant lecture tour in America.[26]

The book in which Gertrude Stein pondered the question of identity at lengths taxing to the patience of most readers was *The Geographical History of America or The Relation of Human Nature to the Human Mind* (1936), published in the year preceding *Everybody's Autobiography* and only three years after the appearance of *Alice B. Toklas*. As intimated by her subtitle, Gertrude Stein posited a distinction between identity and "entity" corresponding to Plato's duality of being and existence but reversing Plato's terms.[27] Being (in time and in relation to others) is a function of human nature; existing (outside of time) is a function of the human mind. Gertrude Stein's name for the relationship, or lack of it, between these two states was "being existing," and the second was clearly the higher.[28] Thus she advised:

> Beware of be.
> Be is not what no one can be what no one can see and certainly not what no one can say.
> Anybody can say be.
> Be is for biography.
> And for autobiography.
> No not for autobiography because be comes after.
> So once more to renounce because and become.[29]

In Gertrude Stein's scheme, being and existing are associated with complementary personalities or selves: there is the I identified by and with human nature and susceptible to memory and change of circumstance; and there is the I of the mind or consciousness that "knows what it knows and . . . has nothing to do with seeing what it remembers."[30] The first I is not interesting because its nature "resembles the nature that any human beings have"; it is an anybody.[31] The second I is both more personal and more impersonal. It comprehends the inviolate inner self and simultaneously, in Thornton Wilder's phrase, "gazes at pure existing."[32] When this second I knows without being aware that it knows, it resembles Emerson's Man Thinking; it is an everybody. Because this essential self is changeless and timeless and so "eternally young," Gertrude Stein asked a question that suggests why her autobiographical writings could never take the form of an education.[33] "But what is the use of being a little boy if he is going to grow up to be a man," comes up almost as often in *The Geographical History* as Gertrude Stein's constant references to her little dog. "Do you see what a mistake it is to say that," she asks.[34]

The purpose of Gertrude Stein's treatise on self-existence appears to have been to affirm her inner integrity and to convince herself that "entity" existed apart from identity: "I am I has really nothing to do with the little dog knowing me, he is my audience, but an audience never does prove to you that you are you."[35] Gertrude Stein wanted to believe this because she feared that in writing *The Autobiography of Alice B. Toklas* she had sacrificed her inner I to audience demands and the rewards of popular and commercial success. "Be" had no place in "autobiography," not merely because it came after "A" in the alphabet but because it came after "auto" (for "autogenesis," perhaps?). A *bio*graphy was a story of identity, and "identity is history and history is not true because history is dependent upon an audience."[36] An *auto*biography to be "true" should be an inside narrative about the life-giving entity that exists prior to reductive accounts of life-events. Yet in *Alice B. Toklas*, she had written a memoir (hostile readers might consider it a tale of people-who-have-known-me) that one critic later dismissed as mere "chitchat."[37] The book was hardly that; it was a highly artful, perhaps classic, American autobiography drawn with much greater economy than some of Gertrude Stein's more self-indulgent portraits. But it was undeniably a history of being in times and places and among people glamorous enough and even once scandalous enough to have attracted an audience more interested in the bohemian Gertrude Stein than in her writing. Had that audience created her? The popular lecturer and dispenser of *mots* to the daily press who made a sensation on her American visit in 1934–35 had reason to wonder. And there was no denying that *Alice B. Toklas* went against Gertrude Stein's avowed principles of composition. It appeared to be a work of human nature. Whether in atonement or not, Gertrude Stein followed it with a work of the human mind. *Everybody's Autobiography* did not win a large audience and probably never will, even though it is more interesting technically than *Alice B. Toklas* and more typical of Gertrude Stein's other work.

I

The Autobiography of Alice B. Toklas properly begins with the photograph on the frontispiece captioned "Alice B. Toklas at the door."[38] Since it pictures Gertrude Stein in the foreground (however dimly visible at a table) and Miss Toklas in the background (however sharply outlined in the light of an open door), the photograph hints at a secret not to be revealed fully until the last paragraph of the book—the narrative to follow will center on Gertrude Stein, it is really her autobiography. Less evident perhaps is the fact that the photograph also clarifies Alice Toklas's function in "her" narrative. She will open the door for us into the taper-lit sanctums, the pavilion and atelier at 27 rue de Fleurus, where Gertrude Stein wrote and where she officiated over the fair courts of art and the *vie de Bohème*. Thus it is fitting that the first two chapters of her story establish Miss Toklas's credentials as a guide. (Hereafter the fictional Alice Toklas will be called simply "Alice.")

The brief "Before I Came to Paris" identifies Alice as a native of Gertrude Stein's adoptive California who is qualified by birth to be her companion in the staunch Americanism Gertrude Stein maintained throughout the years in France. We learn too that Alice is interesting in her own right. She is "gently bred" and fond of domestic pleasures—needlework, gardening, paintings, furniture, tapestry, houses, and flowers. But there is nothing of the mere functionary about her; like James's Brooksmith, she indulges an exacting taste for excellence, and we are early alerted to her later acquisition of "three first class geniuses"— Gertrude Stein, Picasso, and Alfred North Whitehead (pp. 3, 6). Alice will not be awed by these figures, however, for her outlook is toughened by the disciplined whimsy and ironic wit suggested by her well-known remark, "I like a view but I like to sit with my back turned to it" (p. 3). No ordinary young woman, she is launched into the rue de Fleurus by a San Francisco earthquake like the one that heralds birth and rebirth at the beginning and end of Lincoln Steffens's autobiography. Fire following the quake of April 1906 brings the Michael Steins home to assess the damage, and Alice is lured away by Mrs. Stein's stories of Paris life and her three Matisse paintings. "In this way," she says, "my new full life began" (p. 6).

The chapter entitled "My Arrival in Paris" is as close as Gertrude Stein will come to writing a story of education. Surrogate to her hostess as well as guide for the uninitiated reader, Alice must be acclimated to her new life by degrees. For the time being, she is another American innocent abroad. "Now I was confused and I looked and I looked and I was confused," she says upon first seeing the paintings in Gertrude Stein's atelier (p. 12). There is, however, a great deal to be known when innocent Alice arrives in 1907. The first paragraph of chapter 2 explains that she has dawned upon Paris at a key moment in the history of the cubist movement. Matisse has just finished *Le Bonheur de Vivre*, and Picasso is working on a "complicated" picture of female figures that may have been the revolutionary *Les Demoiselles d'Avignon*. Moreover, Gertrude Stein is seeing *Three Lives* through the press and again writing away at *The Making of Americans*. She has but recently finished sitting for Picasso.

Cast into the midst of all this, Alice senses a fullness in the Paris life that is heightened in the ensuing pages by Gertrude Stein's tactic of placing Alice in moments of concentrated activity that are passed off as daily routine. Alice is introduced in rapid succession to the picture-laden atelier, dinner in the pavilion along with the Picassos, and one of Gertrude Stein's "evenings," where she is invited to the opening day of the Independent Salon. The *vernissage* of the Independent is to become for Alice what the Louvre was for Henry James (who once dutifully replied to nineteen-year-old Alice Toklas's written suggestion that he dramatize *The Awkward Age*). Sitting before two paintings that seem to attract more attention than all the rest, she is told by Gertrude Stein: "Right here in front of you is the whole story" (p. 22). For Alice as for the equally puzzled reader, explanations must wait until she has gained more knowledge of her new milieu. But already at the *vernissage*, Alice is shedding her innocence. She soon becomes "more accustomed" to the people, and even some paintings are growing familiar (p. 24). Among those by Matisse she is "beginning to feel at home" (p. 21).

Gertrude Stein, of course, has been at home among such oddities all the while, and her intent in chapter 2 seems to have been not only to arrange Alice's introduction to Paris but to show how easily she herself can manipulate the world into which the newcomer is introduced. As Richard Bridgman has pointed out, she treats Matisse, Picasso, and lesser artists as "inspired children" who must be humored but hardly idolized.[39] She sends Picasso into ecstasies of gratitude with a present of Katzenjammer Kids comics. At a luncheon, she makes all her guests happy by the simple device of seating each painter across from his own work. And she knows when Picasso and his mistress have parted by watching for Fernande to pawn her earrings. By such evidence of superior cunning, we are prepared to accept Gertrude Stein as more than a spectator when Alice promises at the end of the chapter to "tell you how two americans happened to be in the heart of an art movement of which the outside world at that time knew nothing" (p. 34).

Alice's hyperbole is apt because it suggests how Gertrude Stein organizes the intensely egoistic third chapter describing her entrée into the Paris art community during the years 1903–7. This fine section ostensibly takes form around three paintings that are the structural equivalents of the paintings that would reveal "the whole story" to Alice in chapter 2 if she only knew enough to understand them. But Gertrude Stein develops her own connection with each of the paintings in such a way as to make herself the heart or magnetic center of both the chapter and the cubist movement.

The first painting is a Cézanne portrait, pertinent here not because Cézanne was a forerunner of cubism but "because in looking and looking at this picture Gertrude Stein wrote Three Lives" (p. 40). (The other model for *Three Lives*, according to Gertrude Stein, was Flaubert's *Trois Contes.*) The second painting is Matisse's *La Femme au Chapeau*, bought by the Steins for about one hundred dollars at the Salon d'Automne in 1905, the same year Gertrude Stein met Picasso. The story of its acquisition leads to one of the most effective pieces of narrative portraiture in the *Autobiography*, a description of Matisse, his wife, and daughter that resembles a sketch by de Maupassant without the ironic twist. The episode is supposed to celebrate the triumph of Madame Matisse's perseverance in holding out for the asking-price of the painting, but it has the effect of making Gertrude Stein the heroine of a little drama of inspired patronage that carries her on to acquire a sample of Picasso's work from the art dealer and former clown Clovis Sagot. In this way she meets the master.

Gertrude Stein and Picasso become fast friends at once; and though Picasso does not normally work with a model, he makes an exception for Mademoiselle Gertrude, who claims to have posed for him ninety times. In the autobiography, the entire winter of 1906 comes back as a season of mere interludes between these sittings. Already established as the patroness whose art collection has attracted so much attention that she must hold open house on Saturday evenings, with this third painting Gertrude Stein is now the subject and inspiration of art as well. The winter of 1906 was very "fruitful," Alice says (p. 66). Matisse painted *Le Bonheur de Vivre*; Gertrude Stein wrote the Melanctha section of *Three Lives* ("the first definite step away from the nineteenth century and into the twentieth century in literature"); and Picasso passed "from the Harlequin, the charming early italian period to the intensive struggle which was to end in cubism" (p. 66).

What is more, she all but asserts, Gertrude Stein was responsible for this last achievement as well. Picasso's struggle is conveyed through his difficulty with the Stein portrait. The demanding task of painting a woman with a "definite impulse then and always toward elemental abstraction" stimulates Picasso's "spanish quality of ritual and abstraction" (p. 78). Further influenced by African sculpture, to which he has been introduced by Matisse to whom he has been introduced by Gertrude Stein, Picasso will later achieve the fierce distortion of the "primitive" figures in a painting like *Les Demoiselles*. And Gertrude Stein will publish her first major book, *Three Lives*. From serving as patroness and then model for other artists, she has passed quickly to creating art of her own.

In the meantime, Alice the narrator has also changed. While recalling events from the years before she met Gertrude Stein, Alice almost fades into nothingness, the flimsiest of veils for Gertrude Stein's own presence. But as the chapter approaches 1907, the year Alice came to Paris, she reappears with a new-found knowledge of her hostess. As if brought up to date by the disclosures of the years before her arrival, she now understands the significance of the two paintings that puzzled her at the independent art show: by frank imitation, they "publicly showed that Derain and Braque had become Picassoites and were definitely not Matisseites" (p. 79). Henceforth, the best talent will be attracted to the "school" of Picasso. Matisse's influence in the narrative will wane as Picasso and Gertrude Stein grow more intimate. And at the beginning of the next chapter, Alice will assume the part of "one of the habitués of the rue de Fleurus" (p. 85).

Indeed, Alice is now so completely in possession of her subject that she can double back to fill in the history of "Gertrude Stein Before She Came to Paris." Beginning with Gertrude's birth in Allegheny, Pennsylvania, in 1874, chapter 4 quickly recalls Amelia Stein's falling-out with her sister-in-law, the family's removal to Vienna and France, and their return around 1879 to America and California, where Gertrude Stein lived until the family dispersed in 1892. Then, somewhat more fully, Alice turns to the years at Radcliffe during which Gertrude Stein "had a very good time" and to the years at the Johns Hopkins Medical School, where she was frightfully "bored" (pp. 95, 100). She closes with 1903, the year Gertrude Stein joined her brother Leo in the rue de Fleurus.

In addition to placing the past on record, this short chapter revives the generational theme of *The Making of Americans*, a book to which it several times alludes. It demonstrates that though Gertrude Stein's circumstances have changed through the years, her basic personality has not. In the photographs bound with the first edition of the autobiography, the strangely aged little girl stiffly posed in boots and sash above the caption "Gertrude Stein in Vienna" is a more solemn miniature of the robed woman pictured before the atelier door. Had she grown up to be a different person, as the little boy threatens to do in *The Geographical History*, there would be no point in telling about her. The *Autobiography* rests on the assumption that everything touching the mature Gertrude Stein (at the height of her powers and holding intellectual sway over the celebrities who attend her evenings) is inherently interesting. This is why, having reminded us of Gertrude Stein's comment to Ernest Hemingway that "remarks are not literature," Alice nonetheless punctuates the chapter with Gertrude Stein's sayings, as for example: "She always says she dislikes the abnormal, it is so obvious. She says the normal is so much more simply complicated and interesting." (Pp. 94, 102.)

The effect of "1907–1914," however, is to confirm Gertrude Stein's remark to Hemingway about remarks. Chapter 5 too often falls short of "literature" because Alice is unable to sustain the gaiety and momentum of the earlier chapters. Occasionally lapsing into gossip, she seems at a loss to know what to do with Gertrude Stein once she has established her hostess's importance and her own authority as a witness. Part of the problem, as Richard Bridgman has analyzed it, "is that Alice Toklas can no longer give a direct, personal account of either herself or of Gertrude Stein. The stages of her increasing intimacy with the writer, and the estrangement from Leo were both privileged information. These were memoirs, not confessions. A little of the stress and affection of the two women's friendship is made discreetly visible, but the passion, the quarreling, and the despair that churn through Gertrude Stein's other writing are absent."[40] Her readers had to be willing to accept a degree of holding back as Gertrude Stein's price for her otherwise absorbing disclosures. That she withheld more than a little proved she had never been entirely the creature of her audience, despite her worst misgivings.

Furthermore, chapter 5 develops Alice's character in contradistinction to Gertrude Stein's. We learn among other things that she is sometimes clumsy and will not tell what she has broken until Gertrude Stein agrees to have it mended; that she once expressed a "violent" preference for Avila over her friend's beloved Paris; that she at first would not watch bullfights until Gertrude Stein told her when not to look. And, most important for the internal arrangement of the chapter, we learn that the fictional Alice's life revolves around her friend's Saturday evenings.

Although this portion of Alice's narrative too often collapses into brief, apparently random paragraphs like the entries in a diary, the chapter derives a certain unity from the controlling metaphor Alice assigns to her life in Paris. "It was based," she says, "upon the rue de Fleurus and the Saturday evenings and it was like a kaleidoscope slowly turning" (p. 109). The image of the kaleidoscope perfectly describes the fragmentation of this chapter and the years it covers. Perhaps it was merely a coincidence, but Alice had chosen one of the habitual metaphors of Gertrude Stein's favorite teacher. William James's *Principles* more than once mentions the kaleidoscope and nowhere more notably than in the chapter on "The Stream of Thought," where it figures as a metaphor for the consciousness:

> As in a kaleidoscope revolving at a uniform rate, although the figures are always rearranging themselves, there are instants during which the transformation seems minute and interstitial and almost absent, followed by others when it shoots with magical rapidity, relatively stable forms thus alternating with forms we should not distinguish if seen again; so in the brain the perpetual rearrangement must result in some forms of tension lingering relatively long, whilst others simply come and pass.

A few lines later, James states the conclusion his metaphor is intended to serve: "Properly they are but one protracted consciousness, one unbroken stream."[41]

Chapter 5 immerses us in the unbroken stream of Alice's consciousness of the Paris years, thus testifying to Gertrude Stein's greater interest in the continuity of consciousness set forth in James's theories than in the idea of incessant change also implied in James's "stream." And since Alice's consciousness of the past is evoked at the time Gertrude Stein writes (the oft-mentioned "now" of October–November 1932), chapter 5 reverts to the "continuous present" of *The Making of Americans* just as it anticipates the principal narrative method of *Everybody's Autobiography*. At the end of the chapter, Alice's kaleidoscope ceases to turn not because she drops it but because the stability of the old Paris life is broken by Leo Stein's departure and by the approach of war. New wallpaper plus the addition of electricity and a covered passageway between pavilion and atelier in the spring of 1914 signify that 27 rue de Fleurus will never again be quite the same. Says Alice, the "old life was over" (p. 175).

In the final two chapters of the *Autobiography*, Alice carries the history of her friendship with Gertrude Stein through the war years and the era of the lost generation into the early 1930s. The ultimate effect of the war upon the two friends is to make the old life of Saturday evenings impossible. When the war breaks out, Alice and Gertrude Stein are stranded in England at the home of Alfred North Whitehead (Alice's third genius). Finally able to return to Paris, the two women experience a sense of tremendous relief: "We were once more at home" (p. 191). But Paris is changing, and the war is made real to them by a zeppelin alarm that causes Alice's knees to knock together "as described in poetry and prose" (p. 194). For a time, Alice and Gertrude Stein try to escape the war by retiring to Palma de Mallorca; this time when they return, it is "to an entirely different Paris" (p. 207). Everywhere are signs of the war effort, including an American girl driving a Ford marked "American Fund for French Wounded" (p. 207). It is Alice, not Gertrude Stein, who responds with decision: "There, said I, that is what we are going to do" (p. 207).

Gertrude Stein has a Ford truck ("Auntie") sent over from America, she learns to drive it, and the two women join the A.F.F.W. as sisters of all work. They leave Paris for Perpignan, Madame Matisse's old home district, and for a new active way of life without any stable center. They become military godmothers; they distribute "comfort bags" to the troops; they have themselves photographed with the Ford and print post cards that are sent to America to raise funds; they assist at hospitals, aided by Gertrude Stein's medical training; they transport wounded soldiers; and when the armistice comes, they see the trenches and help with the refugees. As chapter 6 ends, Alice and Gertrude Stein are spectators at the great victory parade down the

Champs Elysées and through the Arc de Triomphe. Not only have they "once more returned to a changed Paris"; they must find a new stability in "a restles and disturbed world" (pp. 233, 234).

After the war, as described in the final, seventh chapter, Alice and Gertrude Stein try to resume a version of the prewar Paris life; but, as Alice observes, the "old crowd had disappeared" (p. 237). There is, however, an endless flood of new faces. Alice remembers the advent of T. S. Eliot, Ezra Pound, Sherwood Anderson, Scott Fitzgerald, Lincoln Steffens, Jo Davidson, Djuna Barnes, Glenway Wescott, Robert McAlmon, and, of course, Ernest Hemingway. Even though Alice's memory of them is often confused, visits from these men or conversations about them occasion some of Gertrude Stein's most entertaining and sibylline remarks in the *Autobiography*. She contends "that Sherwood Anderson had a genius for using the sentence to convey a direct emotion . . . and that really except Sherwood there was no one in America who could write a clear and passionate sentence" (p. 268). Fitzgerald, she is sure, "will be read when many of his well known contemporaries are forgotten" (p. 268). And she accuses Hemingway of being "ninety percent Rotarian. Can't you, he said, make it eighty percent. No, said she regretfully, I can't." After all, she and Alice agree, Hemingway "does have moments of disinterestedness" (p. 270).

The roll call of Gertrude Stein's guests along with Alice's need to refer to "the bibliography of Gertrude Stein's work" to refresh her memory of the postwar years suggest a subtle difference between this and earlier chapters and between Gertrude Stein's acquaintanceships before the war and after (p. 237). Most of the visitors and friends mentioned in chapter seven are not painters but writers, and Alice seeds the chapter with the titles of Gertrude Stein's books (especially *The Making of Americans*, finally published in 1925, over fifteen years after its composition). More than any preceding, this is a "literary" chapter; and it has the same aim as Madame de Clermont-Tonnerre, who says to

Gertrude Stein a few pages from the end, the "time has now come when you must be made known to a larger public" (p. 307). Having long been her companion and friend, Alice is now Gertrude Stein's publisher; thus she advertises her client's work and attempts to convince readers that Gertrude Stein is more than a personality: she is a producer of literature. Hence all the references to Gertrude Stein's publications, to her "english success" in lecturing at Cambridge and Oxford in 1925, and to the French translations of her work, adduced to show that her "reputation among the french writers and readers was steadily growing" (p. 306). Alice's greatest feat as a publisher, in the root sense of the word, is to write an autobiography that is actually a biography of her friend. "She" succeeds so well in this that we are not much disturbed to be told at last that Gertrude Stein has been her own publicist. And we are all the more charmed with the deception since Gertrude Stein (or is it Alice B. Toklas?) has written her autobiography "as simply as Defoe did the autobiography of Robinson Crusoe" (p. 310).

II

The implications of Gertrude Stein's allusion to *Robinson Crusoe* as the model for *The Autobiography of Alice B. Toklas* are practically limitless. Crusoe's first-person account of his adventures is generally considered to be a secularization, in fiction, of the Puritan spiritual autobiography.[42] It contains the usual evidence of providential grace in the miraculous appearance of barley corn outside Crusoe's cave; and it stages a traditional conversion scene when Crusoe, emerging from a delirious fever, scans the New Testament, realizes the vileness of his past sins, and cries out for deliverance. The narrative is "secularized" because of Crusoe's (and possibly Defoe's) belief that the rewards of Providence come for services rendered and have a material value. Crusoe merely goes through the motions of being saved; his spiritual epiphany does not really transform him, for afterward, instead of eternally giving thanks, he goes off to survey the island. Crusoe's main concern, and the interest of the narrative for most readers, is with matters of utility—how to get his salvage ashore, how to bake bread and build a dwelling. The story of Crusoe's kind of economy (rather different from Thoreau's) is of particular importance in the history of American autobiography because Benjamin Franklin was an avowed admirer of Defoe and because *Robinson Crusoe* helped establish the tradition in which Franklin wrote his *Autobiography*.

Certainly much of the interest of *The Autobiography of Alice B. Toklas* comes from Gertrude Stein's remarkably specific attention to her surroundings and to the business of daily life in the rue de Fleurus. To a degree, the book is another narrative of utility and function. We are told in minute detail what the inside of Gertrude Stein's atelier looked like; that it is opened by one of the few Yale keys in Paris; that Gertrude Stein's notebooks are the kind with pictures of earthquakes and explorations used by French schoolchildren; that her note paper and napkins are stamped with the device "a rose is arose is a rose"; that she can drive a car forward well enough but has trouble backing. And so on. Assuming her subject to be inherently interesting, Alice correctly assumes that we are curious about everything connected with Gertrude Stein, however, quotidian; and Gertrude Stein's published acknowledgments of her debt to Defoe likewise suggest that we are to read the autobiography for its documentary appeal. Her statements about Defoe usually concentrate, however, on how *Robinson Crusoe* is narrated. It is the *simplicity* of Defoe's narrative that she is trying to imitate, according to the last paragraph of *The Autobiography of Alice B. Toklas*. In one of the four essays collected in *Narration*, she adds this longer though scarcely simple "clarification": "Think of Defoe, he tried to write Robinson Crusoe as if it were exactly what did happen and yet after all he is Robinson Crusoe and Robinson Crusoe is Defoe and therefore after all it is not what is happening it is what is happening to him Robinson Crusoe that makes what is exciting every one."[43]

If Gertrude Stein seems to be groping for her meaning here, it is because she probably was. Elsewhere in the same lecture she lumped together, as kindred forms, newspapers, history, biography, and autobiography; and she defined narrative as a way of telling about "what is happening all the time": "Narrative is what anybody has to say in any way about anything that can happen has happened and will happen in any way."[44] By this measure, *Robinson Crusoe* and *The Autobiography of Alice B. Toklas* are genuine narratives because they convey "happenings" (people doing things) as any good memoir must. But what about the dominant tense of the two books? Do they convey what is happening or what has happened or both? This was where Gertrude Stein's explanations hedged. In *Narration* she wanted to locate the action of *Robinson Crusoe* in the present. Defoe's account of "what did happen" was an account of "what is happening" to Crusoe each new time a reader opens the book. But Gertrude Stein classified *Crusoe* as an autobiography, and she linked autobiography with biography and history, which "concerns itself with what happens from time to time."[45]

In *The Geographical History of America*, completed after the Chicago lectures, Gertrude Stein no longer placed autobiography and biography in the same category of narrative. "Be" was all right for biography, but not for autobiography; autobiography had to do with existing. And in the earlier lectures, she had distinguished between "existing and happening."[46] With narratives of existing, the narration is internalized and divorced from time because the "events" it describes are always going on. Conversely, narratives of happening are external and timebound. Thus when she came to write *Everybody's Autobiography* (and partly as a result of thinking through *The Geographical History*), Gertrude Stein realized that her earlier assessments of what she had done in *Alice B. Toklas* had been inaccurate by the terms of her own theory. The narrator of *Everybody's Autobiography* recalls saying to Thornton Wilder (with whom Gertrude Stein liked to discuss problems of narration) that she had not succeeded in telling her first autobiography "simply," though she knows what the process entails: "I would simply say what was happening which is what is narration."[47] Gertrude Stein had been mistaken in thinking she had written this kind of narrative: "The first autobiography was not that, it was a description and a creation of something that having happened was in a way happening not again but as it had been which is history which is newspaper which is illustration but is not a simple narrative of what is happening not as if it had happened not as if it is happening but as if it is existing simply that thing" (pp. 302–3). Where she had managed to do "simply that thing," she said, was "in this book"—*Everybody's Autobiography* (p. 303).

There is little point in embarking here upon a full-scale reading of the book in which Gertrude Stein realized her notion of how autobiography should be written. Much of the interest of *Everybody's Autobiography* comes from its illustration of a theory, and *Alice B. Toklas*, no doubt, will continue as the autobiography that interprets Gertrude Stein to most readers. Yet our concern here is with the directions, however extreme, in which American autobiographers of the twentieth century pushed their forms. Gertrude Stein went to greater extremes than most; and since her most extreme and original contribution to the genre lay in narrative method, we should consider *Everybody's Autobiography* at least briefly in that aspect.

The five major divisions of *Everybody's Autobiography* anticipate or follow from Gertrude Stein's lecture tour in America (October 1934 through May 1935); but chronology is even less important here than in the earlier autobiography. From the opening pages, it is evident that a different principle of narrative organization is operating. Consider this sample:

> Alice B. Toklas did hers and now anybody will do theirs.
> Alice B. Toklas says and if they are all going to do theirs the way she did hers.
> In the first place she did not want it to be Alice B. Toklas, if it has to be at all it should be Alice Toklas. . . . Alice Toklas never thought so and always said so.

That is the way any autobiography has to be written which reminds me of Dashiell Hammett.

But before I am reminded of Dashiell Hammett I want to say that
just today I met Miss Hennessy and she was carrying, she did not
have it with her, but she usually carried a wooden umbrella. This
wooden umbrella is carved out of wood. . . . When it rains it does
not open and so Miss Hennessy looks a little foolish but she does
not mind because after all it is the only wooden umbrella in Paris.
And even if there were lots of others it would not make any difference.

Which does remind me of David Edstrom but I have been reminded of him after I was reminded of Dashiell Hammett. (P. 3)

This passage and the narrative that follows are written in what
The Making of Americans called "the continuous present":
"anybody creating anything has to have it as a present thing,"
says the author of *Everybody's Autobiography* (p. 34). And in
this second autobiography the present is more present, as it were,
than ever: "In The Making of Americans I was making a continuous present a continuous beginning again and again, the way they
do in making automobiles or anything, each one has to be begun,
but now everything having been begun nothing had to be begun
again. Now I am writing about what is which is being existing"
(p. 251). This way of writing autobiography depends primarily
upon the free association of ideas in the present consciousness
of the narrator. Thinking of Alice Toklas's autobiography reminds the narrator (call her Gertrude) of autobiographical method in general, and thinking of that reminds her of Dashiell Hammett (because autobiographies and detective stories have much
in common), and thinking at all reminds her of Miss Hennessy's
umbrella because it (or the memory of it) has "just today" been
thrust into Gertrude's consciousness.

Thus *Everybody's Autobiography* reproduces Gertrude's
stream of thought, and we should read the book as Leon Edel
has suggested we read a modern psychological novel: "not as a
time-sequence but as a heterogeneous series of perceptions
each catching its moment of intensity without reference to what
lies on the succeeding pages."[48] In the intensified continuous

present, time is what Virginia Woolf in *The Waves* called "the unlimited time of the mind" and what Faulkner described as "a fluid condition which has no existence except in the momentary avatars of individual people." For Gertrude Stein as for Quentin Compson, "there is no such thing as *was*—only *is*."[49]

It is tempting to assume that Gertrude Stein's continuous present derives from such time-philosophers as Henri Bergson and her friend Alfred North Whitehead, whose work expressed the same concepts of the internalized perception of time that were reshaping the modern novel. But John Malcolm Brinnin is probably correct in denying that Gertrude Stein was ever a true Bergsonian.[50] *An Introduction to Metaphysics* indicated that Bergson's concept of duration was grounded in memory as an active agent. "Without this life of the past continuing into the present," said Bergson, "there would never be any duration, but only instantaneousness."[51] In *The Geographical History of America*, Gertrude Stein proclaimed that the human mind had nothing to do with remembering; for her, instantaneity was all. This is why the continuous present of *Everybody's Autobiography* and of segments of *The Autobiography of Alice B. Toklas* differs in a fundamental way from Sherwood Anderson's "moments" in *A Story Teller's Story*. For Anderson, the past is forever recapturable because it survives in the present; Gertrude Stein forswears memory and obliterates all distinctions between past and present in one, eternal Now. She was a cubist; Anderson was something else; and his moments more closely resemble those of Proust, "whose characters," as Donald Sutherland has said, "are protean and live in a perpetual metamorphosis, a sort of creative evolution, not only as families or genera but as individuals."[52]

The years of intimate acquaintance with the cubist movement in painting may account for Gertrude Stein's fascination with the continuous present; but she could have come to it even earlier through William James. James's chapter on "The Stream of Thought" listed among the five "characters" of thought two potentially conflicting principles. "Within each personal consciousness," he wrote, "thought is always changing."[53] (It was perhaps this emphasis on the transitive nature of thought that later prompted James to consider mind as a relation or function rather than the entity of the *Principles*.) According to James's second principle, however, "Within each personal consciousness thought is sensibly continuous": he can never have exactly the same thought at two different times, but Peter wakes up in the morning and knows that he is Peter and not Paul.[54] Most of Gertrude Stein's work is an application of this "character" of thought, including *Everybody's Autobiography*—which concludes with this answer to the self-doubts raised in *The Geographical History*: "perhaps I am not I even if my little dog knows me but anyway I like what I have and now it is today" (p. 318). Gertrude Stein had found the perfect story of "existing" in the account of her native country's lionizing a writer who, by writing an autobiography, had finally come into her own.

Although Gertrude Stein's theory of autobiography led to narratives of existing rather than of becoming or becoming educated, those narratives were not intended to be static. One who always had an appetite for objects, Gertrude Stein did not bring the outside inside because she wished to retreat into a contemplative inner world cut off from "Human Nature." She conceived of existing as a state of continuous motion or mental vibration in which the consciousness passionately appropriates the objects of its detached contemplation. She was, in effect, a metaphysical poet, a true student of the William James who used "think" and "feel" interchangeably. Creature of inertia though she claimed to be, Gertrude Stein tried to contain the movement and fragmentation, the fads and machines, of her kaleidoscopic age. Thus Henry Adams would have been justified in taking her for a modern incarnation of the female force he thought enclosed the universe no longer. It is fitting that Jo Davidson's statue of Gertrude Stein resembles a female Buddha (or a more robust sister of the asexual figure on the Adams tomb) who looks fully capable of embracing the twentieth century instead of renouncing or transcending it.

Like all theories of autobiography, Gertrude Stein's assumed a theory of human nature: our "emphasis and the moment in which we live changes," she once said; but "we inside us do not change."[55] Most of the portraits after "Ada" (1909)—and her autobiographies are but extended portraits—illustrated Gertrude Stein's belief that we each have a "bottom nature." On the strength of such remarks, we might seem justified in regarding Gertrude Stein's self-portraits as throwbacks to those chronicles of the timeless self written by Thoreau, Franklin, and even Daniel Defoe. Each of these writers had assumed for his fictive "I" a bottom nature that remained stable enough to lend its form to the universe that each had discovered within himself or had made in his own image. The life stories of such natures, when shaped by time at all, had traced the growth or cultivation of character from what Sampson Reed called "an internal principle." In the language of Gertrude Stein, these autobiographies had assumed that "nothing changes from generation to generation except the composition in which we live."[56] Franklin and Thoreau had differed not so much in their basic views of human nature as on the question of whether the art of composing the world around themselves was essentially imitative or creative, mechanistic or organic. Both had believed that the "we" remained more or less constant, and *Walden* had even located Thoreau's fully expanded ego in something resembling the continuous present.

To the generation of Henry Adams and Mark Twain, however, the self appeared to be defined more by external forces than by internal principles. Their generation's autobiographies followed the ego's history in its struggle to adjust to the multiplicity of a world that William James described as "pluralistic." These accounts of how one man educated or failed to educate himself to live among complexities were necessarily time-bound, and they tended to assume a linear configuration—whether that line was divided into segments, as in Adams's case; broken in halves, as in Clemens's; or pieced out to give the illusion of continuity, as in Howells's and James's. Even when this generation felt the pull of internal rather than external forces, they were seldom comforted. The recesses of memory and the chaotic lower levels of consciousness, to which memory gave access, seemed more often disturbing in their threat to self-integrity than soothing in their promise to alleviate the fearful responsibility of self-definition.

The wilderness of the mind was to seem less threatening, if no less wild, to the generation of writers in America who helped create the modern psychological novel. The antithesis of repressive forms, Anderson's narrative moments and Gertrude Stein's continuous present were modes of self-expression and release not unlike Mark Twain's free-flowing autobiographical dictations. In them, the chronology of the education form was replaced by psychological time, and the linear development of character gave way to timeless being. Instead, however, of actually reverting to the egocentricity of Thoreau or Whitman, Gertrude Stein embraced the multiplicity of her times by achieving the abstraction (rather than concentration) of the self toward which Henry Adams had been moving in the *Education* and which he later abandoned because of its dispassion. Even more confidently than Anderson, she assumed the role of the new Newton whom Adams called for in his *Letter to American Teachers of History*; her passionate detachment, she claimed, was peculiarily American and peculiarly modern. The essence of being an American in the twentieth century, said Gertrude Stein, was to respond to "the vitality of movement":

> In short this generation has conceived an intensity of movement so great that it has not to be seen against something else to be known, and therefore, this generation does not connect itself with anything, that is what makes this generation what it is and that is why it is American, and this is very important in connection with portraits of anything.[57]

The new autobiography as Gertrude Stein wrote it expressed not the centripetal motion of Thoreau's excursions or Whitman's tramps but the *centrifugal* motion of the mass-produced Ford car, the airplane, and the flat American landscape without boundaries or obstacles that air travel revealed to her. Such movement, she felt, could not be captured even in linear stories of personal adaptation to changing circumstances. Only autobiographies of "being existing" fit the conditions of modern life. Gertrude Stein asked us to remember, in the three narratives she considered worth mentioning in her generation, that "there is, in none of them a story. There is none in Proust in The Making of Americans or in Ulysses. And this is what you are now to begin to realize in this description I am giving you of making portraits."[58]

1. Ella Winter and Herbert Shapiro, eds., *The World of Lincoln Steffens* (New York: Hill & Wang, 1962), p. vii.

2. *The Autobiography of Lincoln Steffens* (New York: Harcourt Brace, 1931), p. 710. *The Autobiography of Lincoln Steffens* is copyright 1931 by Harcourt Brace Jovanovich, Inc.; copyright 1959 by Peter Steffens. Reprinted by permission of the publishers. Subsequent citations from the *Autobiography* are to this edition and will appear in parentheses in the text.

3. Ella Winter and Granville Hicks, eds., *The Letters of Lincoln Steffens* (New York: Harcourt Brace, 1938), p. 1051.

4. *The World of Lincoln Steffens*, p. vii.

5. "Lincoln Steffens: He Covered the Future," *Commentary* 13 (February 1952): 147.

6. Ibid.

7. In a letter to his publisher written in April 1930 as he was working on the final chapter of the *Autobiography*, Steffens proposed several alternate titles. "But I find," he added, "that I still prefer the original 'My Life of Unlearning' " (Winter and Hicks, *Letters*, p. 869).

8. *The Education of Henry Adams*, 2d ed. (Cambridge, Mass.: Houghton Mifflin, 1918), p. 88.

9. Gold is quoted in Daniel Aaron, *Writers on the Left* (New York: Harcourt, Brace & World, 1961), p. 189.

10. See Hicks, "Lincoln Steffens: He Covered the Future," p. 153; *The World of Lincoln Steffens*, p. 68.

11. Quoted in *The World of Lincoln Steffens*, p. 68.

12. *Lincoln Steffens: A Biography* (New York: Simon & Schuster, 1974), pp. 270, 271.

13. Ray Lewis White, ed., *Tar: A Midwest Childhood* (Cleveland: Press of Case Western Reserve University, 1969), p. 10.

14. *A Story Teller's Story* (New York: Huebsch, 1924), p. 309. Succeeding references to this edition appear in parentheses in the text. *A Story Teller's Story* is copyright © 1924 by Sherwood Anderson. Renewed. All quotations are reprinted here by permission of Harold Ober Associates Incorporated.

15. Ray Lewis White, ed., *Sherwood Anderson/Gertrude Stein* (Chapel Hill: University of North Carolina Press, 1972), p. 42.

16. Rex Burbank, *Sherwood Anderson* (New York: Twayne, 1964), p. 118.

17. Howard Mumford Jones and Walter B. Rideout, eds., *Letters of Sherwood Anderson* (Boston: Little, Brown, 1953), p. 43.

18. James Schevill, *Sherwood Anderson: His Life and Work* (Denver: University of Denver Press, 1951), 287.

19. Winter and Hicks, *Letters*, p. 366.

20. *Sherwood Anderson*, p. 343.

21. *Education of Henry Adams*, p. 385.

22. Winter and Hicks, *Letters*, p. 33.

23. Anderson's "idealistic" conception of realism comes out in statements like this from *A Writer's Conception of Realism*: "The life of reality is confused, disorderly, almost always without apparent purpose, whereas in the artist's imaginative life there is purpose . . . to give . . . form—to make it true and real to the theme, not to life" (quoted in David D. Anderson, *Sherwood Anderson: An Introduction and Interpretation* [New York: Holt, Rinehart & Winston, 1967], p. 152).

24. *Gertrude Stein in Pieces* (New York: Oxford University Press, 1970). p. 235.

25. *Everybody's Autobiography* (New York: Random House, 1937), p. 85.

26. Quoted in Bridgman, *Gertrude Stein in Pieces*, p. 235.

27. *What Are Masterpieces*, ed. Robert Bartlett Haas (New York: Pitman, 1970), p. 86.

28. Allegra Stewart has unraveled the technicalities of "this increment of depth in existence" in *Gertrude Stein and the Present* (Cambridge, Mass.: Harvard University Press, 1967), pp. 29–67. At one point (p. 30), however, she seems to equate being with "an individual's entelechy," leaving as the other term "his life history (his 'existing')"; this apparent reversal of Gertrude Stein's terms is "corrected" on p. 33 when she writes, "For Gertrude Stein, therefore, *to be* anything meant *to exist*, in a certain way, in relation to time and identity. . . ." And she adds the necessary caveat that Gertrude Stein "avoided the purely Platonic notion of eternal Being divorced from actuality" (pp. 33–34). Gertrude Stein's "existing" was exempt from the control

of actuality, yet it was a state not of transcending but of *experiencing* all actuality.

29. *The Geographical History of America or The Relation of Human Nature to the Human Mind* (New York: Random House, 1936), p. 156.

30. Ibid., p. 27.

31. Ibid., p. 63.

32. Ibid., p. 8.

33. *What Are Masterpieces*, p. 90.

34. *Geographical History*, p. 118.

35. Ibid., p. 77.

36. Ibid., p. 111.

37. B. L. Reid, *Art by Subtraction: A Dissenting Opinion of Gertrude Stein* (Norman: University of Oklahoma Press, 1958), p. 186.

38. Subsequent references to *The Autobiography of Alice B. Toklas* (New York: Harcourt, Brace, 1933) will appear in parentheses in the text.

39. *Gertrude Stein in Pieces*, p. 222.

40. Ibid., p. 227.

41. *The Principles of Psychology* (New York: Holt, 1890; rpt. 1918), 1:246, 248.

42. See G. A. Starr, *Defoe and Spiritual Autobiography* (Princeton: Princeton University Press, 1965), pp. 74–125.

43. *Narration: Four Lectures by Gertrude Stein* (Chicago: University of Chicago Press, 1935), p. 45.

44. Ibid., pp. 30, 31.

45. Ibid., p. 30.

46. Ibid., p. 38.

47. *Everybody's Autobiography*, p. 302. Subsequent citations in parentheses in the text are to this 1937 first edition.

48. *The Modern Psychological Novel* (New York: Grosset & Dunlap, 1964), p. 137.

49. Virginia Woolf is quoted in Morris Beja, *Epiphany in the Modern Novel* (Seattle: University of Washington Press, 1971), p. 36. Malcolm Cowley, ed., *Writers at Work: The "Paris Review" Interviews* (New York: Viking, 1958), p. 141.

50. *The Third Rose: Gertrude Stein and Her World* (Boston: Little, Brown, 1959), pp. 300–302.

51. L. E. Bassett, trans. (Boston: Luce, 1912), p. 53.

52. *Gertrude Stein: A Biography of Her Work* (New Haven: Yale University Press, 1951), p. 11.

53. *Principles*, 1:225.
54. Ibid.
55. *Lectures in America* (New York: Random House, 1935), p. 195.
56. Ibid., p. 165.
57. Ibid., pp. 173, 166.
58. Ibid., p. 184.

Index

Adams, Henry, ix, x, 5, 10, 12, 18, 19, **27–48**, 117, 118, 120, 133, 134, 135, 137, 142, 149, 175, 176, 177; advice of, to Henry James on writing biography, 28; as originator of the education form, 21; career of, compared with Clemens's, 51–53; dynamic theory of history of, 37, 42; essay of, on John Smith, 34; life of, divided into phases, 39; loss of faith of, in evolutionism, 34–35; lost adolescence of, 55–56; marginal notes by, in James's *Principles of Psychology*, 46; mechanistic sense of history of, 56; nostalgia of, 54; pessimistic determinism of, 44, 45; phase theory of history of, 41, 44; philosophical idealism of, 44; psychological theory of history of, 44; search for continuity by, 22; threat of psychological determinism to, 53; views of, on consciousness psychology, 47

—works: *Democracy*, 74; *The Education of Henry Adams*, **27–48** (as shield of protection, 28; author's dissatisfaction with, 27–28; *Confessions* of Saint Augustine as model for, 28–29, 30–32, 43–44; dialecticism of, 31–32, 43–44; egocentrism of, 45; Gibbon's influence upon, 30, 36, 37; history and autobiography coincide in, 35, 41; influence of New England climate upon, 32–33; influence of Rousseau's *Confessions* upon, 28–29, 30; irony of, 29; Manichean heresy of, 33; as model for *A Story Teller's Story* [Anderson], 144–49; psychological determinism of, 46, 48; romance form imposed upon, 30–31; seasons as emblems of disjuncture in, 33; shaped by Adams's phase theory, 35–42; suspense as rhetorical strategy in, 33; threat of unconscious in, 46; wave metaphors in, 37–38); *History of the United States*, 52; *A Letter to American Teachers of History*, 47, 177; *The Life of George Cabot Lodge*, 146; *Mont-Saint-Michel and Chartres*, 41, 146; The "Rule of Phase Applied to History," 36, 37, 39, 43

Adams, John, 34

Adams, John Quincy, 34

Adams, Marian (Mrs. Henry), 51

Afraja (Mügge), 95

Alcott, Amos Bronson. See *Human Culture*

Aldrich, Thomas Bailey, 78, 130; *The Story of a Bad Boy*, 65

American Journal of Psychology, 20

Anderson, Irwin, 144, 146–47

Anderson, Sherwood, x, 126, **138–56**, 168,